Amazing Imagination

Edited By Wendy Laws

First published in Great Britain in 2023 by:

Young Writers
Remus House
Coltsfoot Drive
Peterborough
PE2 9BF
Telephone: 01733 890066
Website: www.youngwriters.co.uk

All Rights Reserved
Book Design by Ashley Janson
© Copyright Contributors 2023
Softback ISBN 978-1-80459-859-7

Printed and bound in the UK by BookPrintingUK
Website: www.bookprintinguk.com
YB0561J

Foreword

Dear Diary,

You will never guess what I did today! Shall I tell you? Some primary school pupils wrote some diary entries and I got to read them, and they were **EXCELLENT!**

Here at Young Writers we created some bright and funky worksheets along with fun and fabulous (and free) resources to help spark ideas and get inspiration flowing. And it clearly worked because **WOW!!** I can't believe the adventures I've been reading about. Real people, make-believe people, dogs and unicorns, even objects like pencils all feature and these diaries all have one thing in common – they are **JAM-PACKED** with imagination!

Here at Young Writers we want to pass our love of the written word onto the next generation and what better way to do that than to celebrate their writing by publishing it in a book! It sets their work free from homework books and notepads and puts it where it deserves to be – **OUT IN THE WORLD!**

Each awesome author in this book should be **SUPER PROUD** of themselves, and now they've got proof of their imagination, their ideas and their creativity in black and white, to look back on in years to come!

Contents

Appleton Wiske CP School, Appleton Wiske

Dylan Bateson (8)	1
Sophia Bateson (11)	2
Isabelle Heald-Orton (8)	4

Beehive Preparatory School, Redbridge

Ismael Chishti (8)	5

Birchills CE Community Academy, Walsall

Keandre Kanthunkako (8)	6
Teodora Serbanesca (9)	8
Jameela Alhassan (9)	9
Mazinah Kousar (9)	10
Amina-Noor Aftab (8)	11

Bury & Whitefield Jewish Primary School, Unsworth

Joshua Davies (8)	12
Daisy Canter (7)	14
Jaeden Hussain (8)	16
Adina Korn (10)	17
Sophia Goldstone (8)	18
Edie Powsney (8)	19
Kimberly Brace (10)	20
Darcie Joseph (9)	21
Serena Leigh (10)	22
Max Goldstone (10)	23
Laythen Lester (7)	24
Shmuli Scherer (10)	25

Cubitt Town Primary School, Isle Of Dogs

Maryam Hussein (10)	26

Newberries Primary School, Radlett

Harishh Nimalakamar (8)	28
Freya Goodman (8)	30
Dylan Finn (8)	31
Olivia Miller (8)	32
Noah Harris (8)	33
Katie Shapiro (8)	34
Coco Colman (8)	35
Leonidas Jenkins (8)	36
Rita Cerqueira (8)	37
Kimia Normohammad (7)	38
Nina Fedorek (8)	39
Georgie Mitchell (8)	40
Kai Brough (8)	41
Daniel Blain (8)	42
Lydia Campbell (8)	43
Alyssa Torrence (8)	44

Queen Boudica Primary School, Colchester

Sophie Kearey (8)	45
Serrah Abeesh (8)	46
Ivy Partridge (7)	48
Arfa Minhas (8)	50
Max Andrejevic (8)	52
Sharen Gnanavel (7)	54
Hazel Robin (8)	56
Emily Kearey (8)	58

Andrew Anish (8)	60
Helba Sanoop (8)	62
Ciyanna Nyika (7)	63
Sophia Kelly (8)	64
Alex Farook (8)	65
Chase Songhurst (8)	66
Henry Eckardt (8)	67
Dixie McLeric (8)	68
Manahil Zaki (8)	69
Lucas Kulich (8)	70
Antonio Kurion (8)	71
Joseph Hurley (8)	72
Freddie Gillespie (8)	73
Sophia-Mae Caunter (8)	74

St Barnabas' CE Primary School, Pimlico

Angelique Bass (8)	75
Louis Howard (8)	76
Aun Kazmi (8)	78
Huda Ali (8)	79
Zain Al-Sammak (8)	80
Miki Minagawa (8)	81
Ryusei Katoh (8)	82
Emily Howard (8)	83
Ciaran Clancy (8)	84
Aiya Iqra Miah (8)	85
Humaira Begum (8)	86
Hudson (9)	87
Michael Jon David (8)	88

St George CE Primary School, Great Bromley

Donovan Finlayson (9)	89
Isla Wilkinson (9)	90
Antoni Strzelczyk (8)	93
Caleb Taylor (9)	94
Elsie Abraham (9)	97
Charlie Batts (9)	98
Sienna Worn (8)	100
Isabella Rivas Long (9)	102
Lilly Jeffery (8)	104

Maddie Bateman	106
Emily Wainer (9)	108
Maya Varma (9)	110
Lily-Rose Stoian (9)	112
Millie Brown (8)	114
Alfie Giles (9)	116
Poppie Usher (9)	118
Melody Duffield (8)	120
Emily Brewer (8)	121
Fred Card (8)	122
Sebastian Lord (8)	123

St Mary's Catholic Primary School, Bognor Regis

Ray Johnson (10)	124

Wansdyke Primary School, Whitchurch

Jenson Kelly (9)	125
Holly Saunders (10)	126
Poppy Rossiter (9)	128
Danika Newell (10)	130
Amina Kallamoqi (9)	132
Jenson Ashman (9)	134
Harry Barrett (10)	136
Starla James (10)	138
Annalise Quirks (10)	140
Dolly Lewis (9)	142
Lilah Taylor (10)	144
Max Stenning (10)	146
Effy Coombs (10)	147
Stan White (10)	148
Roux Harris (10)	149
Spencer Dix (10)	150
Izzy W (10)	151
Evan Hudd (10)	152
Tessa Bowering (10)	153
Reno Lacey (9)	154
Libby Pope (10)	155
Reid Griffiths (10)	156
Hallie Thompson (10)	157

Woodlands Community Primary School, Upper Cwmbran

Indie Williams (10)	158
Evie Rostron (10)	160
Calon Griffiths (11)	161
Holly Furness (11)	162
Maddison Williams (11)	163
Jack Higgs (10)	164
Lola Ralph (10)	165
Neve Eyers (11)	166
Ffion Mason (11)	167
Ethan Watkins (11)	168
Rylee Alexander (11)	169
Ellie Titcombe (11)	170
Caleb Owen-Smith (10)	171
Rhys Evans (11)	172
Riley Parfitt (10)	173

The Diaries

Mbappé's Diary

Dear Diary,
I'm Mbappé and I am a really good footballer. I'm only 24 years old. Today we played against Bayern Munich. The match started and I was dribbling and I scored. I was screaming with happiness. Next, it was the final but Muller scored. I was so annoyed. Then it was penalties. Neymar had the first one and scored. I scored and we won the Champions League. I lifted the trophy and did my celebration.

Dylan Bateson (8)
Appleton Wiske CP School, Appleton Wiske

A Day In The Life Of An Evacuee

4th September 1939

Dear Diary,

Today may be the day I see my family for the last time. When I heard the news about the evacuation on the wireless, I was very scared and anxious. I packed my suitcase. I had pyjamas, a night-time teddy, socks, plimsolls, my ration book, a toothbrush, a towel, clothes, a bar of soap, a handkerchief and a gas mask in case the Germans drop any bombs. Will the war ever end?

My little sister and I met up with the rest of the school at the train station. Snakes wriggled around in my stomach. The train arrived and it was very old and rusty and the windows had fingerprints all over them. The train took a long time to get to the countryside since it was so far away. I'm very relieved that I am with my little sister so I can look after her. We finally got to our new home. I feel apprehensive and nervous about being with new people. Will they like me? We went into a line and our new parents chose people they wanted to keep based on strength and how they looked. Thankfully, my sister and I got chosen to stay together since we were both tall and strong. Even

though I'm scared that I'm away from my family, I'm glad I'm away from all of the fire and fear. Will I see my family ever again?
Got to go, see you tomorrow.
Anne.

Sophia Bateson (11)
Appleton Wiske CP School, Appleton Wiske

Wolf's Adventure

Dear Diary,

My name is Wolf. I am a horse, wild and strong and the leader of my team. I am the king of the mountains, ruling all the rivers and valleys. Today I saw a squirrel stuck in a hole. I panicked and ran to get a rope. I let it down and he climbed out. "Thank you," said the squirrel.

Now we are the best of friends. We galloped into the mountains and all of us felt free together.

Isabelle Heald-Orton (8)
Appleton Wiske CP School, Appleton Wiske

The Ambush

Dear Diary,

I have had many adventures, but this is the one where I truly became a hero. The post I was put on was small; it only had five troops. Yep, five. We were meant to buy time for the eastern defences to get ready for the attack. Then I received a call. "At main camp, they're having a party at 00:00. Good luck, bye," said the phone call. Just then, I was attacked. The Noob (Jaiden) died first and killed no droids. The Averages (Anad and Musa) killed thirty-three. The Pros, Ismael R and Riaz, killed thirty-three each. We'll win. So, we did just that and we won. We came in time to go to the party.

Here I am now, writing the diary as the commander of the first Royal Legion. There were 10,000 droids...

Ismael Chishti (8)
Beehive Preparatory School, Redbridge

Crime Fighting - The Time Jerker

Dear Diary,

My name is Henry Hart and I am seventeen years old. My sister, Piper, is thirteen years old. Ray is thirty-five years old, Schwoz is forty-one years old, Charlotte is fourteen and Jasper is fifteen.

Every morning two minutes before 7am Ray Triple beeps me. Today when I answered my watch he said, "Good morning to you, welcome to Wednesday. Your face looks like poo," in a singing voice.

I asked, "What's up?"

Ray said, "We're so close to capturing the Time Jerker."

I was shocked and said, "Seriously, no kidding?"

"Henry, can you leave school and help?" Ray asked.

I started to panic and said, "No," because I couldn't leave the test Schwoz had set but then Ray and I blew a bubble and transformed into Captain Man and Kid Danger. I used my hypermobility and punched him really fast. Captain

Man is indestructible and punched the Time Jerker and he was fully knocked out. The crime fight was complete!

Keandre Kanthunkako (8)
Birchills CE Community Academy, Walsall

Cindy's First Day Of School

Dear Diary,

Today has been the best day of my life because it was my first day of school! Words aren't enough to explain my wonderful experience. I always wanted to know how school felt and it is actually amazing. I met my new kind and caring teacher, Mrs Rachel. There are thirty children in each classroom and in total 270. My friends are Katy, Danny, Max and Rexi, they gave me gifts to welcome me. In my opinion, the school is very huge because we have a cafeteria, nine classrooms, two playgrounds, one car park (big) and a garden. The school perimeter is 333 metres.

Anyway, the children and teachers are very kind and so is the principal. If you are wondering what subjects I did they are... English, reading, maths (it was awesome), break, art, lunch and computing, that's loads I know for a day. We have PE tomorrow and my favourite is rugby. I like rugby but I don't know if it's going to be tricky or easy but just in case it is hard I'm going to practise.

Teodora Serbanesca (9)
Birchills CE Community Academy, Walsall

The Gone Town

Dear Diary,

It was an early warm morning last Saturday, that was the day that me and my parents went to Wales throughout the weekend. The coolest part of all was that we rented a private apartment only for us. When we finally arrived there, unexpectedly the weather suddenly changed. We got a tour around the colossal apartment instead of Wales. I rushed to the master room and I jumped on the huge bed with excitement. But something caught my attention, it was a massive wardrobe built into the wall. I opened it and there was nothing except dust and a little suspicious handle. A handle? I decided to open it. Before I knew I had already passed the portal. The bright sun made me feel blurry. All of a sudden I saw a signboard in the sky saying 'Gone Town'.

Jameela Alhassan (9)
Birchills CE Community Academy, Walsall

My Mean Sister And Her Coloured Paper

Dear Diary,

Today I used my sister's coloured paper to make a poster for my school project, but my sister found out I took paper from her workbook and she hid it away from me because she said it was the only paper she had left.

This made me sad, I wish my sister would be nice and if it was the last sheet she would give it to me because I am the smallest child, but my sis says I cannot take her things without her permission.

My mum saw I was sad and said, "I have bought you your own coloured sheets so you can make your own posters."

This made me happy, finally my sis and I now have our own colouring sheets so we don't have to share.

Mazinah Kousar (9)
Birchills CE Community Academy, Walsall

Sarah And The Bully

Dear Diary,

It has been a dreadful day today. Sit comfortably as I tell you my story. I was with my friend Erica in the playground when the class bully Selma came up to me and she kept calling me Sarah the ugly bear and bug-bitten scrap. I was getting very upset as everyone was laughing at me.

In class, Miss Thopmore asked me why I was crying but I didn't say a word. Erica then blurted out, "Miss Thopmore, Selma called Sarah names!" "Selma, come here. You need to stop. Face the wall and don't look at anybody!" said Miss Thopmore. At lunch, Selma said sorry which made me feel a bit happier.

Sarah.

Amina-Noor Aftab (8)
Birchills CE Community Academy, Walsall

The Accidental Time Traveller

Dear Diary,

I went on a trip to Uganda. We were on a holiday for nine days. The time it took to get there was thirteen hours and forty-five minutes. It was enormously fun.

At first when we got here, the people made fun of my snake patterns on my arm. Eventually they got used to it. Some people thought it was even a bit cool.

On my fourth day I went to a place where you could put one foot on the northern hemisphere. It was so exciting. I went with my grandma.

In a minute, suddenly there was a blue circle. It sucked me in. One thing I knew though, I was no longer in Uganda. All my friends were about the age of my parents. I was in the future! I felt very overwhelmed and confused! The place I was in now was Russia. It had taken me to the other side of the world. Was I a kid or an adult? It turned out I was thirty.

I needed to get back. How could I? A stranger then told me I couldn't get back. He was big and cruel. He hit me. I think he wanted a fight. I grabbed a gun. I put it by his head. Then he finally told me how to get back. "Turn the handle and go forward."

There were only ten minutes before the land was destroyed. I couldn't get out. I heaved as hard as I could but then I felt so tired. Soon everything went dark...
The next thing I knew I heard my alarm clock go off. I sat up in bed confused. Was it all a dream?

Joshua Davies (8)
Bury & Whitefield Jewish Primary School, Unsworth

Angel The Fairy

Dear Diary,

Today was really boring and frustrating. Do you want to know why? Well, today I went to school (fairy school) and it was very fun until maths. You won't guess what we had to do! We had to do Roman numerals and I am only in Year 3! I have never learned Roman numerals in my life.

A second later the maths teacher said that 10 is x and I was listening but she told me I wasn't. She was a teacher and I didn't want to be rude so I agreed with her.

The next lesson was art, I love art. I am very good at it, in fact, at my last school I was the leader of the school art club which was extremely fun. Anyway, in art we drew a picture of Axel Scheffler. A second before we finished art, the teacher pointed out that the artist Axel Scheffler did books with Julia Donaldson.

When I got to the cooking classroom, Mrs Branspot was there writing down a cookie recipe. I was very confused because the recipe didn't seem right. Maybe because it had the word subtraction in it.

Anyway, that's enough talking for today. Goodnight, Diary, see you tomorrow evening. I hope you have some good dreams.

Daisy Canter (7)
Bury & Whitefield Jewish Primary School, Unsworth

My Surprise Family Holiday

Dear Diary,
It was 6am and my mum shouted, "Surprise!"
I couldn't believe it. "What's going on, Mum?" I asked.
Mum replied, "We are going to Spain."
"What now?" I asked.
"Yes, the taxi will be here in thirty minutes," Mum said excitedly.
I couldn't believe it, I was so ecstatic, I felt like it was my birthday all over again.
We finally got off the aeroplane and we straight away got a taxi to the most magnificent hotel which was on the beach. I took my shoes off and walked across the hot sand. Me and Zakey built the most amazing sandcastle whilst eating the most delicious blueberry ice cream.
The next day we went to the best theme park ever, where we got to ride the scariest roller coasters ever!
On the third day we rode in a hot-air balloon and I saw the most beautiful landscapes ever.
On the last day we went to a water park and I screamed, "This is the best holiday ever!"

Jaeden Hussain (8)
Bury & Whitefield Jewish Primary School, Unsworth

The Breakdown (Sunday)

Dear Diary,

I had a wonky day today. Let me dig in and I will tell you about my day. Let's get into it...

In the morning I decided to have breakfast in the garden and do some of my homework. My homework was so boring that I fell asleep during it but I really needed a nap because I went to bed very late last night.

After that I had a break from homework and then I made it to my friend's house to drop off a gift but she insisted on me staying for two hours so I gave in and said only for two hours and no more because I had to finish my homework.

Halfway through the hour, she started saying, "You always get everything you want!" and this is when she started to have a breakdown.

I calmed her down but she started not to like me for what I had done over the years. I said that none of that was true and she finally calmed down and I got some silence.

Adina Korn (10)
Bury & Whitefield Jewish Primary School, Unsworth

The Great Escape

Dear Diary,

Today was the great escape! Smirks and I had noticed after Sophia fed us that she left the lid off our tank so we waited forever to see whether they would come and put the lid back on but they didn't! That's when we planned our great escape... We slowly climbed up the mountain and the plants until we got to the top. Soon we were in a massive bubble together and it was taking us somewhere. Then we saw a cage but it was not like our cage, it had lines in. Smirk was so excited. I was nervous, just in case we got caught.

Simon then opened the cage and we floated in, it was like a miracle. We met the gerbils Alvin, Simon and Theodore. They were very nice.

Suddenly, oh no... Sophia spotted us and she carried us back into our tank safely. We are not doing that again!

Sophia Goldstone (8)
Bury & Whitefield Jewish Primary School, Unsworth

My Embarrassing Moment

Dear Diary,

Yesterday I arrived at my bestie's house. Edie lives in Bury and I live in South Manchester so it's an hour away. There was a street party going on and we were having a sleepover. We were going to play Truth or Dare? which is a game where you either choose a dare or answer a question.

Now here comes the exciting bit... When we were playing the game I chose to ask her if I could kiss her. Guess what she said, "Of course!" So I went in and kissed her. I couldn't believe it, my parents would never let me do that! After that, we went to bed.

A few hours later and it was breakfast time. Edie's mummy was making pancakes so I showed her how to make mermaids. It was all so enjoyable!

Edie Powsney (8)
Bury & Whitefield Jewish Primary School, Unsworth

My Wonderful Day Out

Dear Diary,

Today I went to the most amazing park with Kimberly my owner. It was the best. It was full of crunchy leaves that went under my tiny paws. There were loads of trees and it was amazing.

My owner gave me treats when the rest of the family were having a delicious-smelling picnic. Kimberly is the best because she gave me an extra treat!

After a long, tiring walk, I rested for about an hour and then played with Kimberly. First, we played tug of war and then we played fetch.

After a while, it was time to go to bed and Kimberly lifted me gently into bed. I fell asleep comfortably on my back with my paws in the air. Oreo.

Kimberly Brace (10)
Bury & Whitefield Jewish Primary School, Unsworth

I Just Wanted Friends

Dear Diary,

Yesterday I came out of the ocean, my natural habitat to go and find a new place to settle. I went and you won't believe it, I found a crystal cave. I went in and found some mummies dressed in stuff that I wipe my butt with.

Thinking it was a dream, I said goodbye to them and well, it meant hello. So I asked to be friends with them but all they did was laugh, saying, "Never would we be seen with you!" It made me so sad but mainly unwanted,

I have to go back to the ocean. I'll see you tomorrow and hopefully I won't be so terrified.

Darcie Joseph (9)
Bury & Whitefield Jewish Primary School, Unsworth

The Time I Got Trapped By A Venus Flytrap

Dear Diary,

I was on a walk and I was in the forest. It was a magical forest. I came along to a big treehouse and walked inside. Inside was a Venus flytrap. I got swallowed up and it felt gooey and sweaty and then I got spat out. I was confused about where I was. I had the decision to go left or right. I went right and hoped it would be the right way. All of a sudden, I got to my house but it started to thunder a lot but at least I was home.

Serena Leigh (10)
Bury & Whitefield Jewish Primary School, Unsworth

Sushi And Tofu

Dear Diary,

Today I got a new companion. She told me her name was Tofu! She doesn't have a dorsal fin, shocker!

Tofu swims like she is drunk. Don't know why! She even swam into the glass today! I think she's partying too hard at night!

Anyway, Tofu has settled in well and we both like the same food. We also adore peas!

Next time I think I will be prepared when the next fish comes along!

Max Goldstone (10)
Bury & Whitefield Jewish Primary School, Unsworth

Zoo Day

Dear Diary,
I had such a good time at the zoo. There were a few ups and downs but apart from that I had an amazing time. I got to feed the giraffe carrots, stroke the animals and feed the lemurs fruit. There was also a fun park and I went on one of the rides. I didn't know what a zipline was but it was really fun. My mum and dad had a coffee while I was on it at the beach.

Laythen Lester (7)
Bury & Whitefield Jewish Primary School, Unsworth

The Melted Chocolate

Dear Diary,

As you may well know, I am a chocolate bar. I have just recently been bought and the weather is super sunny. It must be about 38 degrees! "Help!" I keep screaming. I am sizzling and am very scared, anxious and worried. I know I am melting. Thankfully soon they will put me in the fridge so I will not melt.

Shmuli Scherer (10)
Bury & Whitefield Jewish Primary School, Unsworth

Dreaded Destination

Dear Diary,

My name is Lola and I am writing this diary in a boarding school. It all started eleven years ago, when I was born. I was born with a very serious disease. I stayed in hospital for two months before going home. My mother hated me. She said I was cursed and I was a waste of time, but my dad was a whole lot different. He loved me and took care of me. He even took his time to look for a name for me.

At the age of seven, my illness came back and I had to go to the hospital for three months. When I returned, all the pictures of me were in the bin and my room was a mess. It was Mum. At night, I heard this:

"I am sending her away, she is a disgrace!" Mum said.

"You witch!" Dad shouted.

In the morning, Dad got me dressed in fancy clothes and took me somewhere I'd never been before. At the destination, Dad came out and hugged me so tight. He cried and told me that he loved me, and I was taken inside as I watched him on his knees.

As I sit here now, I know who is to blame for me being here. Let's just say it's not my dad.
Update soon,
Love, Lola.

Maryam Hussein (10)
Cubitt Town Primary School, Isle Of Dogs

School Trip

Dear Diary,

I was overjoyed when we were going on a super school trip on the 12th of June, 2023. We were going to Verulamium park as massive as a mountain.

First, when I got to the scenic school, we did amazing activities and put our lunches in the colossal coolbox. Soon, we got into perfect partners, I was with Asher and we got into pairs to sit next to each other on the cosy, comfortable coach, as rapid as a roller coaster. As we got on the comfortable coach, it was a loud party!

We walked and I was being a smiling monkey. We hopped elatedly to a huge hypocaust and wrote three amazing adjectives and one super sentence. Soon, we walked to a Roman wall and sketched it, and an elegant, extravagant lake with dazzling ducks.

Then we got into the massive museum and put our bags on pegs, and got into our group. I was with Miss Divine. There were things from 2,000 years ago in a colossal room. My eyes flashed like stars as we saw a lady come in and explain brilliantly the amazing Roman history. We were sitting on tables and changed every few minutes as slow as sloths. First was the dining table where we saw what Romans ate on. I thought it was perilous pottery. Then the kitchen table, where we saw how they cooked. I was amused as I saw a disgusting cow bone. Then was the big building table and we saw what Romans built brilliantly. Lastly was the looking-good table and we saw how Romans looked good. I recognised a lot of things from there.

Soon, we packed our bags and went on the cosy coach. It was amazing, I loved it, it was brilliant. Hope to talk to you soon,
Harishh.

Harishh Nimalakamar (8)
Newberries Primary School, Radlett

School Trip

Dear Diary,

Ten days ago, I went on a spectacular school trip! At 8:15, I got in my mum's electric black car. I arrived at school with all of my kind and inspiring friends. We went on a dark grey coach. I sat next to my friend, Coco. Next, we arrived at Verulamium park and museum at 9:30. First, we saw the dirty hypocaust, it was amazing. I learned that 'hypo' means below and 'caust' means heat. Next, we saw the Roman wall, it was rusty, disgusting and cool. Next, we had five minutes of snacks. After that, we sketched. I sketched the rusty Roman wall. After, we had lunch. After lunch, me and my class had a Roman workshop. We got to touch stuff from Roman times, like olives. They were hard and green. After that, we went back in the dark grey coach, to school. I got picked up by my mum and sister, they asked me loads of questions about how my school trip was. It was the best school trip ever!
Talk to you soon,
From Freya.

Freya Goodman (8)
Newberries Primary School, Radlett

School Trip

Dear Diary,

Ten days ago, we went to the Roman museum. First, we were doing our early-morning walk whilst waiting for the coach when Miss Patrick said that the coach was here! We went outside to see the huge bus. We all got the coach, we drove to the Verulamium museum and park! Me and my friends got off the coach, all of us were excited. So, we entered the park, we went to look for the hypocaust! It looked sick! It was the floor of a Roman home! After that, we had snacks. "Chocolate biscuit, yummy!" Then we saw a Roman wall, it was huge! We sketched the beautiful scenery and found the biggest feather!

Then we had lunch. "Cheese and pickle sandwich, yucky!" Then we went to the Roman workshop and saw a Roman programme, etc, etc... You get it, etc!

Yours sincerely,

Dylan!

Dylan Finn (8)
Newberries Primary School, Radlett

School Trip

Dear Diary,

A few days ago, I went on a school trip. I came to school on a hot, sunny day. I was so excited for the trip. I got on a coach to Verulamium park and museum, then I came off the coach. I was so happy. First, I went to the hypocaust, it means underfloor heating. It was so much fun! After, we had five five-minute snack break.

Then I went to the gigantic Roman wall. I also spotted some ducks in the pond, so I sketched them. Then it was lunchtime! I had a delicious lunch and chatted to my friends. Finally, I went to the workshop, it was very interesting. There were lots of artefacts from two thousand years ago! Then we went on the coach and went back to school. I told my parents how much fun I had.
Talk soon,
Olivia.

Olivia Miller (8)
Newberries Primary School, Radlett

School Trip

Dear Diary,

Ten days ago, me and my friends went to Verulamium park! We were all so, so, so excited! When we were waiting for the coach, we played hangman. I guess 'N', but it wasn't right, and then the coach arrived. When we got on the coach, everybody was so, so, so hot.

Thirty minutes later, we got to Verulamium park, it was boiling hot. None of us were cold! When we got to the park, we sketched the duck pond. Two and a half minutes later, we had lunch. After lunch, we went to the Roman workshop and we saw some things the Romans used. For example, we saw Roman tools and Roman accessories. Then we had a walk around the museum, it was awesome. After that, we went home.

Talk soon,

Noah.

Noah Harris (8)
Newberries Primary School, Radlett

School Trip

Dear Diary,

Tuesday the 13th of June, 2023, me and my classmates went on a school trip to Verulamium park and the Roman museum. First, I got dropped off at school by my mum on a beautiful, bright, sunny day. Second, me and my classmates went to the toilet, grabbed our stuff and hopped on the coach. Me and my classmates got to Verulamium park. Then we went to the toilet. The toilets were so smelly. After we went to the toilet, we saw the Roman floor. After we saw the Roman floor, we saw the Roman wall. It was so cool. We also sketched a lake. The lake was beautiful. Then we had lunch. Lunch was delicious. After lunch, we had a workshop all about the Romans.

Hope to see you soon,

From Katie.

Katie Shapiro (8)
Newberries Primary School, Radlett

School Trip

Dear Diary,

Ten days ago, we went on our amazing school trip at Verulamium museum and park! I felt overjoyed, happy and excited. Here's what happened!

Firstly, we arrived at school, then we all got on the black, grey and white coach and arrived at Verulamium park thirty minutes later. Then we went to the hypocaust (underground heating), ate snacks, went to see an old, broken wall, then sketched under the oak tree, ate lunch, then we had a Roman workshop. I learnt that only rich people could buy mosaics as they were very expensive. We watched a video about the Romans, got back on the coach, we went back to school and our parents picked us up.

Talk soon,

Coco.

Coco Colman (8)
Newberries Primary School, Radlett

School Trip

Dear Diary,

I woke up to a bright, sunny day. I went excited to school because we had a school trip to Verulamium park and the Roman museum. We went on a big, white coach. When we arrived, we saw the amazing hypocaust. Inside, there were fantastic mosaics! Next, we went to the Roman wall, it was brilliant. We sketched a pond and the Roman wall, then we had lunch under a tree. After that, we went to the eye-brightening Roman museum. We got to touch real Roman artefacts! Then we watched a nine-minute clip. Finally, we had a Roman booklet to fill up, then we got our stuff ready to go on the coach for home time.
Talk to you soon,
From Leo.

Leonidas Jenkins (8)
Newberries Primary School, Radlett

School Trip

Dear Diary,

On Tuesday, I went on an awesome school trip to Verulamium park and the Roman museum! After we arrived, we went to the amazing hypocaust with its lovely mosaics. Then we visited the Roman wall and sketched it. I really enjoyed that part! Later that day, we sat down under a tree to have a delicious lunch. When we had all finished, we set off to the museum. When we arrived, I was buzzing with joy because I have never been to a museum. First, we had our workshop about Romans. Secondly, we visited the gallery and saw lots of Roman objects.

I really enjoyed my school trip but, sadly, we had to go.

Talk soon!

Rita.

Rita Cerqueira (8)
Newberries Primary School, Radlett

School Trip

Dear Diary,

A few days ago, we went on a fantastic, super school trip. Firstly, we went on a big, tall coach. I felt happy, excited and joyful on the coach! Then, after the coach, we arrived at a park. That park was called Verulamium park!

It was so much fun. I learned that only rich people could buy mosaics as they were very expensive (mosaics are basically tiles). We saw lots of stuff. We did lots of walking. Then we went to see more things, the Roman artefacts.

Then we watched a movie about the Romans. Lastly, we went back on the coach and went back to Newberries.

Talk soon,

Kimia.

Kimia Normohammad (7)
Newberries Primary School, Radlett

School Trip

Dear Diary,

Ten days ago, I went on an amazing school trip with my class. First, we did some fun Roman worksheets. We gave our good, yummy lunches to our amazing teacher and she packed them up. Then we picked partners and mine was Kimia. We went on the big coach and I sat next to the window. I saw *my flat!* When we arrived, we looked at the hypocaust.

It was suddenly 10 o'clock, so we found a tree and ate our snack under it. We saw the Roman wall and then we ate lunch. We went to the museum and then we went back to school to get picked up.

Hope to talk to you soon,

Nina xxx

Nina Fedorek (8)
Newberries Primary School, Radlett

School Trip!

Dear Diary,

When Miss Patrick said we were going on a school trip to a museum, I felt excited. I felt excited because I wanted to learn more about the Romans. When I went on the coach and in the museum I felt happy to see what they were like. I *love* museums!

At the museum we did a workshop about how the Romans lived. The first thing we did was go to the hypocaust which was an underground heating system the Romans used. Then we had lunch under a tree because it was very hot.

When I got back I felt like I knew more about the Romans.

Talk soon,

From Georgie.

Georgie Mitchell (8)
Newberries Primary School, Radlett

School Trip

Dear Diary,

One day, I was at school and I heard incredible news! I was told that my class was going on a trip, with all my friends! The trip was at Verulamium park and a Roman museum! As soon as I was told about this, I felt like I was going to explode with happiness! When I got home, I immediately told my mum and she was very surprised. She started packing my lunch right away. She made me a chicken sandwich and it looked absolutely delicious!

I had an incredible time!

Talk soon.

Kai Brough (8)
Newberries Primary School, Radlett

School Trip

Dear Diary,

On Tuesday the 13th of June, days ago, we went on our school trip. Our trip was to Verulamium park and the museum. It was a very exciting day. Here it was hot and I was happy. The museum was epic, just like the park was amazing. Sketching was fun.

After lunch, we had a workshop all about artefacts that have been around for 2,000 years. This was the best day ever!

Peace out,

Daniel.

Daniel Blain (8)
Newberries Primary School, Radlett

School Trip

Dear Diary,

On Tuesday the 13th of June, 2023, me and my class went on a school trip. We went to Verulamium park and museum. I didn't expect the toilets to have no toilet roll or no soap. I felt very scared. Then I heard that the boys' toilets were the same.

We went to see the hall and the park. Next, we saw the museum and, next, we had a workshop. It was so fun.

Talk soon,

Lydia.

Lydia Campbell (8)
Newberries Primary School, Radlett

School Trip

Dear Diary,
On Tuesday the 13th of June, 2023, I went on a school trip. I saw beautiful mosaics. I sketched a giant, pretty lake. Then I had delicious lunch. After that, I went to the amazing Roman shop. I saw old, dusty things that were dug up by hard-working archaeologists. After that amazing day, Y3 and I went home.
Talk to you soon,
Alyssa.

Alyssa Torrence (8)
Newberries Primary School, Radlett

The Diary Of Roxie The Black Cocker Spaniel

Dear Diary,

Today was not so good! Firstly my owner shouted, "Come on Roxie, time to go on your walk!" She clipped my lead to my ruby-red collar that said 'Roxie' with shiny silver writing with a bone around it. Then we were off! Down the rose-scented paths, through the tree-lined streets. I then pulled as we passed 'Jollies' my favourite treat shop. I felt the change on my paws from the hot, hard pavement to the cool, soft, freshly-cut grass on the field. My owner let me off my lead. I chased a blue butterfly all the way to the children's playground. I was so excited that I kept running and running. I did not realise that I was in the middle of the road. I was hit by a car. My leg was hurt and was bleeding. Out of nowhere a dog that looked exactly like me came rushing towards me. The dog dragged me to safety out of the road. I had to go to the silly vets. The doggy that rescued me was my mum. Her name is 'Shell'. My owner kept her and got her a matching collar to mine and we lived together. What a day!

Sophie Kearey (8)
Queen Boudica Primary School, Colchester

Sarah And The Magnificent Thing
An extract

Dear Diary,

I am sharing this amazing story with you because I want you to never give up on your dreams. The story is called 'Sarah and the Magnificent Thing'. It all started with a young, inquisitive girl called Sarah, at a park full of smart people. When, suddenly, she saw two women zooming across her, who looked like some scientists with the lab coats and the gloves. They were on flying skateboards and rather than being happy for them since they invented it, she felt jealous because she wanted to make that too. She also felt livid since she knew that she could never be close to that. So, she asked them kindly if she could borrow it for a minute and, thankfully, the first woman said, "Sure, but on one condition."

"You have to look at it in front of us," the second woman explained. Her sentence left Sarah baffled. "Why?" Sarah asked.

"Just in case you'll be ruthless with it," she replied.

The three of them laughed as they handed the flying skateboards to Sarah.
"What are your names?" Sarah asked them.
"My name is Keisha and this is my sister, Cali," Keisha replied.
Then Sarah went to their lab and she had to be honest, the place was so organised! She snapped out of it immediately and she took pictures of the details so she wouldn't forget how it looked. After a serious amount of examination, Sarah took off to her house. Once she reached there, she began to search for all the items she needed, for example, metal, screws, a screwdriver and a lighter.
She stared hard at the details and began to attach and screw the things together.
After one whole hour, she had to admit, it was very hard and when I say very hard I mean it.
Eventually, she gave up as it was too hard, especially with three dogs from Keisha and Cali.
They went to Hawaii for a vacation.

Serrah Abeesh (8)
Queen Boudica Primary School, Colchester

The Incredible Diary Of Patch A Pawsome Pup!

Dear Diary,

Yesterday, Ivy my owner told me that tomorrow there would be a Dogtastic Olympics at Doggy Daycare and I exploded with unstoppable excitement. When it got to bedtime, everyone was asleep except for me as I was thinking about the Dog Olympics and how I would feel if I won a prize. I thought about what I was good at and might win. I am good at tearing paper into shreds and chasing squirrels, pigeons and Midnight the cat who has been stealing my food and making me grumpy!

Dear Diary,

Today was the day. As we drove to Doggy Daycare, I was feeling nervous but mostly excited. Ivy told me to try my best, be a good role model and cheer on the other pups. The first event was limbo and a sausage dog called Kevin won. I felt a bit sad but I told Kevin, "Well done, you did a good job." Then it was catching a ball in your jaws. I came second but no medal. A Labrador called Max won. He is always eating. I was starting to think that there weren't going to be any paper shredding events today and certainly no squirrels to chase. I was feeling disappointed not to have won. Next was swimming. I did not win, but I was happy to be in the water on a hot day with Dave the otterhound who thanked me for my support. Racing was the final event and my last chance to win a medal. I pretended I was chasing Midnight the cat in my garden but Gerry the Greyhound was faster than a speeding car and won the medal.

Deep down I felt a bit sad until at the end of the day the human judges gave me a special award for being the most supportive dog and the best cheerleader. I got a shiny medal and a delicious dog biscuit. I might not be the best runner, swimmer or catcher but I am the best cheerleader in the history of dogs and puppies.

Ivy Partridge (7)
Queen Boudica Primary School, Colchester

Raya And The Demon Unicorn
An extract

Dear Diary,
Today has been an adventurous day for me. It all started like this.
I (Raya) and Little Uni (my teddy) were reading a fabulous history book. We both started a new chapter, 'Akah the Demon Unicorn'. I told Uni, "Look, Uni! We are on chapter ten now." The photographs filled me with curiosity about what Akah looked like or what his magic powers were. Then I was horror-stricken. It said, 'He will return every time after a decade.' He last came when I was born, and now I am ten. I cuddled Uni in fear. I finished the chapter.
I wanted to read more about how to stop him, so I read out loud, "Chapter eleven, Elements of Harmony." As quick as a flash, I read the chapter to find the true answer to my question. At last, I found the answer. To stop him, you have to find the four Elements of Harmony which were happiness, kindness, honestly and generosity. I jumped up and down with joy as I finally knew the answer to stop him.

I raced down to the front door, but when I was about to go out, my mother (Layla) stopped me. She said, "Hello, my honey spark, what are you going to do outside?"
I gulped and mumbled, "*Uhhh*, going to Raina's house to play."
"And how long will that be for?" she asked suspiciously.
"About twelve hours," I replied. "We're having a BUFF (best unicorn friends forever) sleepover," I added.
"*Ohh*, alright. Go on, you don't want to be late, do you?" she said...

Arfa Minhas (8)
Queen Boudica Primary School, Colchester

James And The Maths Exploration

Dear Diary,

Last night, I found the answer to the hardest sum ever and let me tell you what happened. "I'm on the way to school!" I chanted happily. "What puzzle will I get today?" I whispered to myself. I walked to school and greeted my best friends, Max and Jimmy. I asked if they were good and they said yes but Max responded excitedly, "I've got a maths sum for you, it's 2148 x 9272."

"I'll have to work it out," I said puzzled.

So that night I snuck out from home and searched for clues. Eventually, I found a house and on it, it said 'Maths House'. I found silver handles so I opened the creepy door. Inside there was a question that said '3 x 9, is it 1, 18 or 27?' I pressed 27 and a door opened. Next was '99 x 99, is it 3, 8001 or 9801?' I pressed 9801 and it opened. Finally, it said, 'Last question to pass, what is 5200 x 5002, is it 6, 50,000,000,000 or 26,010,400?' I pressed 26,010,400 and the last door opened. Inside, was a floating golden book that had every answer in the world. I picked it up and opened it. I found the answer to the sum!

Later, I ran home, got dressed and went to school. At school, I told Max the answer was 19,916,256!"
"Phenomenal job, James!" Max said as he patted me on the back.
So that's it - Remember, don't ever guess the answers to sums!

Max Andrejevic (8)
Queen Boudica Primary School, Colchester

The Incredible Diary Of Sharen

Dear Diary,
On the 15th of July 1980, I was sitting in the scrapyard waiting for my friend, Rowan to play with me. Clearly, there were not many cars made at this time and the scrapyard had lots of space. I saw a hooded figure lurking about, it had to be him. I ran towards my friend in delight as I took my ball out of my bag, bouncing it towards Rowan. "Wait, where is my ball?" I cried in despair. Looking down, I saw a hole, I jumped into it.
"Wait for me!" shouted Rowan.
When Rowan was with me we sat at a side because there was a dead end. "Argh!" I cried when the walls gave way and Rowan and I fell in. We landed on something soft, a beast, Adrian. The beast yawned as it woke up and started fighting us. Adrian's power was that he could turn people into statues with his mighty claws. While Rowan battled I crept behind the beast, took a piece of chewing gum and stuck it on the beast's leg. As the claws came down to get the sticky thing off I jabbed the claws into the leg. The beast turned into a faded grey as it became a statue. The beast had used his own powers against him!

"Well done!" cried Rowan.

We ran up some steps and found ourselves in the scrapyard again, on the bench I had been sitting on before and there was my ball and a pile of treasure.

We had a great snooze after we looked at the treasure!

Sharen Gnanavel (7)
Queen Boudica Primary School, Colchester

My Magical Birthday!

Dear Diary,

Yesterday was a half-tiring and half-magical day. It was mainly about my birthday, but a fascinating birthday anyone could have. It was 5:30am and dawn was just breaking. The morning sunlight was in my face which made me wake up. Yawning, I slowly got out of bed to brush my teeth. When I got to the bathroom I searched the cylinder-shaped container to find my brush and paste. But no toothpaste and only my brush. Strange! Luckily, I used my mum's toothpaste. After brushing, I stumbled downstairs, wondering if it was too early to wake my parents. I decided it was. I went to the big room but was unlucky to find there was nobody there. Where could they be? I waited for an hour or so and read my book. They still didn't come. I began to worry and decided to go to my best friend Lily's to see if she'd seen my parents. When I got there, the door was open and it was dark inside. Silence greeted me. Suddenly, I felt something touch my shoulder. I turned around and screamed! All the lights turned on and everyone was singing 'Happy Birthday!'

My parents were at the front with a cake and I had the time of my life. Although one thing, the cake icing was my toothpaste so if anyone was to eat that, I'm sure they'd get stomach ache.

Hazel Robin (8)
Queen Boudica Primary School, Colchester

The Diary Of Clover The Cat

Dear Diary,

This is how the best day of my life became the worst! Firstly, I woke up and ate my favourite turkey pouch, it was very tasty and delicious! Then I started to purr on my owner and head rub her.
"Well, hello Clover!" my owner said.
"Meow, meow!" I said.
"Ah! You have lovely pale olive-green eyes!"
It always made me happy when she said that about me. We walked downstairs and my owner let me out. I climbed over the fence and went into the woods as I always did. All of a sudden, I felt something hard on my paws. I looked down and I saw a coal-black gun. I got scared so I ran up a tree faster than a cheetah would! I sensed danger! I saw a person dressed in bright orange clothes with the word 'prisoner' on the back of his T-shirt. I did not expect this to happen on a sunny Sunday morning! Out of the corner of my eye, I glimpsed another ginger tabby cat who looked fierce with razor-sharp teeth and narrowing eyes. Its back was higher than its head and looked like it was ready to pounce. The cat launched itself from the tree behind me onto the prisoner and dug its claws into

his chest. I could not watch the rest of this fight so I tiptoed home to my comfy, soft, warm bed.

Emily Kearey (8)
Queen Boudica Primary School, Colchester

Andrew And The Amazing Beetle Killer

Dear Diary,

Today was a most unusual day! It was a hot summer morning with a warm pleasant breeze when suddenly I woke up. My best friend, Louis was tapping me on the shoulder, as my teacher was approaching me. Fortunately, Mr Elmer didn't shout or get mad with me, but he seemed very grumpy indeed. I must have fallen asleep, as I was drooling and covered in sweat.

As we went outside for our science lesson, I noticed a lanky orange mansion hidden deep within the trees. At first, it was just a tiny speck but as we got closer we realised how big it was. Our science teacher, Mr Lloyd, announced that we were conducting an experiment to see how long frozen juice lasted before it melted. The moment we heard juice we started to lick the mansion but Mr Lloyd didn't mind. As it started to melt beetles surrounded us as they scurried across Newton quickly leapt out of his wheelchair and ran away but due to his allergy to walking he wet his pants. I saw a nearby shop and ran there while my friends fought the beetles. I came back with some beetle spray and attacked the nasty creatures as they fled from us.

Andrew Anish (8)
Queen Boudica Primary School, Colchester

The Unimaginable Unicorn

Dear Diary,

I am telling you this story because I want you to never give up on your dreams. The story is called 'The Unimaginable Unicorn'.

So, once upon a time, a unicorn called AnnRose was hanging out with the other unicorns in the glittery sky, but she kept getting bullied because she was ugly. One night, she was in a deep sleep when a fairy appeared. While she was sleeping, dreaming, there were twinkling stars and a bright light. Suddenly, she woke up and said to the fairy, "Who are you?"

"I am going to solve your problem, but first you have to do three good deeds and then you will become the prettiest unicorn in the world," said the fairy. The three good deeds were, first, show kindness, second, help others, third, lead a truthful life.

After she finished all of the three good deeds, suddenly, she turned into the most beautiful, amazing unicorn in the world. Every other unicorn started admiring her and came to be friends with her. Finally, she became the happiest unicorn in the world.

Helba Sanoop (8)
Queen Boudica Primary School, Colchester

Life As Destiny

Dear Diary,

This is what happened today... It was a normal day and everyone had finished school and work. Then my bestie Leah and I were skipping happily to my house. When we got there we tied our hair up into a cute little bun and I put on my gymnastics uniform and of course, I looked the cutest. That is why I am so popular... LOL! This is when the drama all began. We were all getting ready for the competition which was tomorrow. One of my friends called Izzy said she could do a backhand spring so she did it. One of my other friends called Bella said she could do an aerial so she did one. They were arguing about how they could do it better, so I said I could do both but when I finished I felt a terrible pain! They called 999. They said they had to do surgery on my arm. I told them I felt like a crocodile bit my arm. But it did go well. I am just happy to be alive.

Ciyanna Nyika (7)
Queen Boudica Primary School, Colchester

The Incredible Diary Of The Dancing Girl!

Dear Diary,

Oh hey, I'm Sophia and I am a dancing star, well not when people watch me. I just seem to be that person who never gets ticks, not that I'm not smart. I know 2+2 makes 200, wait no, 900, no 1000, yes that's the answer. Now the reason I made this diary entry is because I'm nervous. I always write in my diary when I'm nervous, it helps me relax. I feel like there's an angry butterfly in my tummy because today is the day of my dance spectacular. Well, it's not that spectacular because I'm drowning in nerves. It's because of the misery of last year's show when my shoe flew off my foot and blasted my teacher in the face. It made me the star of the show... in the worst way, you could think of. Everybody glared their beady eyes at me. I felt completely mortified. Luckily, my teacher is as sweet as icing!

Sophia Kelly (8)
Queen Boudica Primary School, Colchester

A Fun Day With Alex

Dear Diary,

Today I had an adventurous morning. I made pancakes with my mum and after break I went to Strawberry Farm to make strawberry jam because it's Daddy's favourite.

After that, I practised football with my dad. Daddy says my football skills have improved. I can pass and shoot the ball better. I remembered that my coach at Fun Football told me not to stay in a position doing nothing. I should run for the ball and pass to my teammate so I practised, practised and practised until I got better at passing.

After football, I played indoor handball with Amelia and we really enjoyed it. Before I had a shower I decided to have a haircut with Mummy and then I had a cold, fresh shower. I had a delicious warm dinner and finished my homework and read before I went to sleep.

Alex Farook (8)
Queen Boudica Primary School, Colchester

Under The Sea

Dear Diary,
Today I went to the beach and swam with the fish below the water because it was so interesting. The sea was so blue with very clear water. When I explored there was an abandoned shipwreck. When I swam closer it got extremely dark so I put my light on. A shark appeared in front of me so I swam to the top as I got so scared. I managed to swim to shore. I looked back and the shark had vanished into the sea. I found my friend Jack and we played football together. On the beach, I told him everything about the shark and the shipwreck because he wanted to know. Jack wanted to go to the aquarium so we went there. Jack went in the bit with the sharks because he wanted to see a shark. After we went back to the beach and we played volleyball. I won because I was the best player.

Chase Songhurst (8)
Queen Boudica Primary School, Colchester

Mabel And The Golden Treat

Dear Diary,

Today, my dog Mabel and I were out for a walk when Mable found a little dog-sized hole in one particular tree. This tree was no ordinary tree, the leaves were golden and had a glittery tree trunk. Mabel said, "I will come back later!"

Mabel came back but with a torch in her mouth. She went through the rather small hole and when she stepped in she immediately fell to the ground but it became soft so now she had faced the first challenge. She ran across a platform whilst arrows were firing at her, but she dodged them all. When she got there there were golden dog treats and she went darting across the platform and climbed up the ladder out of the hole. As soon as she sat there she immediately became a super dog and was off to save the world!

Henry Eckardt (8)
Queen Boudica Primary School, Colchester

The Incredible Diary Of The Underwater City

Dear Diary,
Today Ocean Bay heard we are going to have a tsunami hit us. Everybody packed, but we were too late. We could see water barging through buildings. I heard yells and screams. I copied other people, running away. Suddenly, I realised how light my body was. It was like an underwater city. Fish swam around cracked buildings and jellyfish covered the sky. Eventually, I swam to the surface when the water cleared. People put up their tents for homeless families. People had food, money and warmth from the tents. Apparently, some of the wooden houses are still standing in the waters far below the ocean. Surprisingly, an epic tsunami is going to return one day and I was going to be looking forward to planning my future.

Dixie McLerie (8)
Queen Boudica Primary School, Colchester

Friends Forever

Dear Diary,
It is really fun to have a best friend, but at the same time, it is really hard to leave them. I love spending time with my friend.
Hey! By the way, my name is Manahil, (you know that) and my friend is Reet.
However, yesterday was the day when I left my friend as our family shifted to UK (Colchester). Both of us were really miserable and full of teary eyes yet both of us were silent.

Dear Diary,
Now I am on an aeroplane and I understand that separation is hard but we have to move on. I am happy that I have you, my wonderful Diary, my best friend forever. You will always be with me whenever I am happy or sad. There will be no separation.
Love,
Manahil.

Manahil Zaki (8)
Queen Boudica Primary School, Colchester

The Incredible Diary Of The Cat And The Mythical Fish

Dear Diary,

I am a cat called Luke. You're probably wondering how a cat is writing a book but trust me this book is all written by my owner Jack. My owner loves me, he's perfect, he gives me strokes, feeds me and plays with me but lately, he has not been interested in me.

I went to the back garden because that's where he was playing. I was shocked by what his new possession was... a fish! His new possession was something he feeds me! I meowed at him to see if he would stroke me but instead, he cried. I know it was a terrible idea but he is only five and I am fifty in cat years. There was only one idea left in my paw...

Lucas Kulich (8)

Queen Boudica Primary School, Colchester

Elis And Holly Planet

Dear Diary,
Today I woke up early and ran outside. The sun was shining. I went about my daily routine: smelling flowers, meowing at other cats and jumping on trees. Suddenly, hidden in the bushes, there was a spaceship and I entered it. After an hour of crazy driving, I reached Holly Planet and crashed into a holly tree. Holly, the cat fell from that tree. We went together to visit Hollylands to get some Holly bread for a Holly picnic.
It was a wonderful time on Holly Planet!

Antonio Kurion (8)
Queen Boudica Primary School, Colchester

The Amazing Diary Of Prez

Dear Diary,
It was my birthday today, November 14th. I celebrated it with my younger sister, Charli and my two mums. Suddenly, a tsunami hit. It tipped over onto the soft yellow sand. The skyscraper moved an inch every time the wind blew. After an hour it was fully in the water, shark-infested water. One by one objects started to disappear. Then one by one people started to go missing too until I was the only one left. A shark came up to me, it was a hammerhead shark...

Joseph Hurley (8)
Queen Boudica Primary School, Colchester

Super Cat And The Animals' Rescue

Dear Diary,

I, Michael the powerful Super Cat, like to fly up to the sky. Today I saw a depressed dog stuck on a massive tree. It had little birds and some owls in there. I then went to the beach to save a rare dolphin with a net on its back and its head. I was angry with the troublemaker for putting nets on a dolphin and dogs in trees. I saw a sheep in the ocean but I couldn't get there quickly enough.

Freddie Gillespie (8)
Queen Boudica Primary School, Colchester

How My Sister Acts Around Me

Dear Diary,

My sister called Freya is very nice most of the time. She lets me play on Roblox and other stuff on her laptop. She is also kind and sticks up for me when I'm getting bullied by people. She tells them to stop being rude to me and they do. But anyway, she is my favourite sister and the best sister ever.

Sophia-Mae Caunter (8)
Queen Boudica Primary School, Colchester

Roba's Life

Dear Diary,
Today was my special day, for me and Anayo. We won everything in the class! We had a dance today, Anayo danced with Tara and I danced with Budo. Anayo was dancing like Wednesday Addams. I was in a red dress. Anayo was in a black dress. We had lots of fun. The music was amazing and, guess what Budo did? Hew flew into a cake during karate club! Ha, ha, ha! That's why you never bring a karate leader into the kitchen when you're cooking and you're powerful.
Yes, I actually beat everyone in the club! It was so funny. *Sigh.* It was so nice, "I love this day!" I am going to go to school again. Someone put a love letter in my locker today: 'At the cherry tree', and it was Budo! He said, "Will you be my girlfriend?" I said, "Yes!"
So, Budo is my boyfriend and he lives with me and Anayo! I will love him forever in my life! I loved this day.

Angelique Bass (8)
St Barnabas' CE Primary School, Pimlico

The Ride Of The Rage

Dear Diary,

I had an excellent day today. I went to Southend. Let me tell you what happened.

We got on the train from Vauxhall, we got off at Southend, Victoria. From there, we walked down the High Street till we got there. Emily (my sister) jumped with excitement, we entered the park. First, we went on the Ferris wheel, we saw big rides, small rides, tall rides. Then I looked at my fear, *The Rage*. We got off the wheel, our mum said, "Will you do it?"

I replied, in a shaky voice, "Okay!" So, we set off towards the ride. Soon, we were there. I watched a few people do it, so I decided I would do it. We sat down in the little cart up the little hill and *whoosh!* Down the drop, did the turn, shot like a bullet right in a loop and, in a second, we came back to the station. I was dizzy, a bit sick and proud I had done it. So, we made our way to the exit and left. We got back on the train, but Emily played up and we got home at 12 o'clock. She would not move an inch. We missed two trains in fifteen minutes. We were just pulling up to ours, we pulled up at Vauxhall station. We got off the train,

on the bus and got off, went home, Emily went straight to bed. I stayed up, put on my pyjamas and went to bed.
We got up in the morning and had had good dreams.

Louis Howard (8)
St Barnabas' CE Primary School, Pimlico

St Barnabas' Tournament

Dear Diary,
Yesterday, it was my best day ever. We won the tournament, so let me tell you about it.
We were getting ready to play our first match, then there was a delay. Then we ran the pitch and back, then it was time. The match began, straight away we were on the attack and we won a free-kick (they fouled us a lot). I was supposed to take it, but Eman took it. He kicked it straight into the wall. A pen was given. Eman took the pen, but Ibrahim was supposed to take it and he missed straight down the middle. Then they were on the attack, but Idress stopped them. Then we were on the attack. Ibrahim passed to Aun, Aun passed the ball to Eman and Eman scored. 1-0 to St Barnabas. That was full-time. Eman scored at the last minute. They were so cocky.
Ten minutes to go and 3-1 down, and I am injured. Eman scored, 3-2. Five minutes to go and Eman scored. Then we got to the pens and we won.

Aun Kazmi (8)
St Barnabas' CE Primary School, Pimlico

The Last Day Of Excitement

Dear Diary,

On the last day of my holiday in Turkey, some people had to come to our villa to clean it because someone else was coming for their holiday. So, we went on an amazing day trip. First, we went to a restaurant to get some soft chips. The first bite I took was as soft as a pile of feathers.

Next, we went to the mosque to pray. It was really big, so my baby sister rolled around on the floor while the rest of us prayed.

After that, we went to the huge shops and we all bought beautiful crystal necklaces and flowery, silver bracelets. Then we ran back to get our suitcases because we left them behind, and then we took a big taxi to the airport at 11pm, and went on the hot plane back to England.

Once we were back in England, we collected our car keys and my dad drove us back home, and we arrived at 1am.

Huda Ali (8)
St Barnabas' CE Primary School, Pimlico

Going Swimming

Dear Diary,

Today, it was an exciting day. I went to go swimming. So, I got ready. I could jump in the pool and hold my nose for five seconds but, suddenly, my nose was hurting a lot when I had to hold my breath. Next, I got out the pool and changed myself. Then we got back home and I was hungry. It was the best day of my life and we got ice cream.

The next day, I went to Battersea park and we played tennis, and I was trying to do it but it was very, very hard to do it. But, suddenly, I scored one point. Then we went back home and I got a haircut. I went back to my bedroom and brushed my teeth and took some water and vitamins, and went to bed and said goodnight to my cousin in Arabic. I read Arabic to them and they said, "Well done, you are so good," and finally I went to bed. Goodnight, I went to sleep.

Zain Al-Sammak (8)
St Barnabas' CE Primary School, Pimlico

The Best Funfair Ever

Dear Diary,

Today was the most fun day ever in my life. I went to a funfair called South End and went on the different types of roller coasters.

First, screaming, I went on a joyful roller coaster. This roller coaster can take a photo if we are scared or not, and I was not scared because I raised my hands up with my friend.

Second, enjoying, I went on a fun, dizzy swing with my friend and we put our arms to the side like a bird or a plane, and we said, "We are flying!" it was fun so I wanted to go on again, but it was a long queue so we decided to go to another one.

Finally, screaming, enjoying, I went on a giant, high roller coaster. I went with my mum, friend and friend's mum. It was very high and so fun. I thought, *this is my best day ever!*

Miki Minagawa (8)
St Barnabas' CE Primary School, Pimlico

Going To Bruges

Dear Diary,

Today was a fantastic day! We went to Bruges. It was so fun! The first day of Bruges was fun! We went to a big restaurant. In the restaurant, we ate some lamb steak. It was very tasty! I ate some fries, they were very, very yummy. Bruges is a city that makes fries! After that, my mum let me have some ice cream. I ate some mango ice cream and watermelon ice cream.

The next day was the last day of Bruges, so we were in a boat and it was a big boat. Then we rode on a horse, it was so fast!

Then we went to France! We went to a big supermarket called 'Monoprix'. It was fantastic, incredible! Then we went to have lunch. We ate snail, we ate pasta, steak and French fries.

Ryusei Katoh (8)
St Barnabas' CE Primary School, Pimlico

A Day At Chessington

Dear Diary,

A while ago, I went to Chessington World of Adventures. It was great; lots of rides.

First, I went to the Jolly Rocker. It was terrifying, I screamed everyone's ears off! It was so loud! That ride was my least favourite one. I hate it. Especially as it was my first ride.

Secondly, I went on the bounce house, it was great. It was slippery and bouncy; that's what made it fantastic. We kept on falling down, then sliding. *Wheee!* We would slip or push each other down.

Third, I went on the carousel, it went slowly. I enjoyed it, and the big rides were far away. I was calm. Well, I did go on the Vampire. That was terrible. Big, bad rides.

Emily Howard (8)
St Barnabas' CE Primary School, Pimlico

Sonic Forces

Dear Diary,

It has been two days since Infinite's attack against Silver and the citizens. Some people have evacuated, then we got an update. The enemy was on the run, retreating to the east. Sonic and Rocky took the highway on Metro.

Double-boosting their way out of the exploding highway, Eggman retreated to his fortress to confront Sonic, Classic Sonic, and Rocky to meet their doom, but destroying the reactor did not stop Eggman.

Three stages, two robots and the one and only Phantom Ruby. The ground was shaking, so now can they defeat Eggman and save the world and more?

Love you, Diary.

Ciaran Clancy (8)
St Barnabas' CE Primary School, Pimlico

The First Day I Was Born

Dear Diary,

The first day I was born, I saw black and grey, but it was day outside. They were so jolly, except my brother. I was so small, 0 years. It was the best day, I'll never, never forget 2015. I don't know anyone except my mum, I love my mum because she's the one who made me alive. She is the only one I trust. I'll never forget her. She's my family. My mum is the best family member ever. She is the best mum! But my siblings are not the best, obviously. My siblings are annoying, but I'm happy I do have them. It was exciting to see my new family.

Aiya Iqra Miah (8)
St Barnabas' CE Primary School, Pimlico

My Kitty

Dear Diary,

On Monday the 20th of February, 2022, my mom gave me, from the adopted centre... *a cat!* My favourite animal. I loved it. At first, she was so nervous but, after a few days, she liked me. She was a Calico cat. I named her Lily. My mom gave me two more cats, Kiki and Lovey Love, Lilly was too playful and jolly. After she licked me, her miaows were so lovely. When I touched her, she was fluffy. I loved her!

Humaira Begum (8)
St Barnabas' CE Primary School, Pimlico

Welcome To Earth

Dear Diary,
Today, I rode in a red rocket. It was exciting.
After a short time, I arrived in a strange country. I was frightened because everything was new.
I was hungry, so I got off the rocket and went to find some food.
I found pepperoni pizza. It was yummy and hot.
Next, I ate vanilla gelato. It was cold and tasty.
Now I am full and happy. I love it here.
From Ben the alien.

Hudson (9)
St Barnabas' CE Primary School, Pimlico

Haaland

Dear Diary,
Haaland scored forty-eight goals in ten seasons. They were the best days of his life.
Because of Haaland, Man City is at the top of the league in the World Cup. Haaland is twenty-three. Haaland always scores, never misses. He made Man City to always win. His team number is nine. When Haaland scores, he always feels the glory. Haaland is the best footballer in Man City.

Michael Jon David (8)
St Barnabas' CE Primary School, Pimlico

The Game

Dear Diary,

Today, I got an awesome plan, it'll just take a bit. I was thinking of finding a shockwave shooter to launch me down and off to a cavern. There's just one problem with that, they are rare, it would be a miracle to get my hands on one.

So, I just need a rest and notice something crazy. In my room, I have a spare shockwave shooter, so out to the cavern I go!

I shoot myself and pack my bags; it's taking a lot longer than I thought, but I had a bat at the magnificent and amazing scenery.

Eventually, after uneventful weeks, I was there! But I heard thunder, rising smoke in the middle of the area. Mind you, I never say that's a very good thing but hey, no wonder I fear for the timing!

Now this is some of the nicest food I've ever had, but the weirdest bit was the amazing heat, until the worst happened. Someone asked, "Are you a visitor?"

I said, "Yes I am," and he shouted, "Intruder!" I ran as fast as I could and hid. I snuck past till I got to the safest place possible...

Donovan Finlayson (9)
St George CE Primary School, Great Bromley

My Dream World

Dear Diary,

I am Lillibet Anna-Clifton, I am twelve years old and I live in London, UK. Recently, I have entered an audition. Not just any audition; an audition for West End's Matilda the Musical, at the Cambridge Theatre! But I am so nervous every time I think about it, it makes me shiver. Oh, by the way, the audition is tomorrow!

Today is the big day, I am currently in my car, my mum is driving me to the theatre!

I've arrived, there are over fifty people auditioning as well! Anyway, I don't care about everyone else; I am just here to focus and win! They call me, it's my time, I say to myself, "There is only one chance, so make it good!"

They say, "Lillibet, you may begin."

I dance for my life, I dance to 'Tattoo' by Loreen from Eurovision. It's over, I have finished the dance. I have exited the stage now; it is not up to me, it is up to them!

It is the next day and I find out tonight! I think I might take a nap for good luck!

"*Echo, Echo,*" I hear a voice. "*Wake up.*" I finally wake up and...

"*OMG, OMG.*" I am famous! But how has this happened; why has it happened? I step out of bed and I am in this amazing room, with a Hollywood mirror and make-up that celebrities wear! I step out of the room, paparazzi are everywhere, I don't know what to do. Suddenly, I just think, *how will I find out about the audition results? Or maybe I don't need to find out the results!* Because I am already famous! "*Aaaaah!*" I can't believe this, I am so happy! I then go back into the room, get changed and walk outside like a superstar. I feel like I am sixteen instead of twelve! Then things get even better. I see my name on the front cover for Matilda the Musical! I wonder where my friends are right now, what about my mum and dad? Oh, I am in a world where my family and friends are not! "*Yesssss!*" I finally get a break! "*Um...*" Guess who I've just seen on the front cover of Kids Vogue? "*This world is just getting better!*"

Then someone comes over to me and says, "What are you doing here?"

I say, "Who are you?"

"Your sister!"

"I don't have a sister though," I say.

"That's what you think, but our mum just didn't tell you because if you knew that you were famous, you would want to come and live in this world. When you were like three, when I left home, you were one so you don't remember me!"
"Well, I want to stay here forever," I say.
"Okay then, but remember, you have to be good."
"Okay."
If you dream it, believe it!

Isla Wilkinson (9)
St George CE Primary School, Great Bromley

Missing

Dear Diary,
There was a gigantic submarine made of broken and old pieces. There were three men on board, they were called Ren, Ciler and Boy. Suddenly, the submarine came off the radar. Everyone panicked. "It couldn't be..." Joey said when he heard the news. He called Jak and James for a mission, an important mission. So, they went to the location. With Jak's brain, they figured out how to survive underwater but it wasn't there, so they swam around. No oxygen. They were doomed. They thought all was lost. Suddenly, they heard something. It was the submarine. They hopped in, but there was loads of water coming in. They got a quick breath, then they saw the three men whose names were Ren, Ciler and Boy. The boys got their magnets and successfully saved them. It was very hard to save them.
Their parents were amazed to see them.

Antoni Strzelczyk (8)
St George CE Primary School, Great Bromley

The Boy In The Dino World

Dear Diary,

It was one ordinary day, then *bang!* Right in the middle of the classroom, a portal appeared. I went inside, then I got thrown out of the other side. I wondered where I was, then I saw a stegosaurus! It was huge. I knew it wouldn't hurt me because it was a herbivore, but I knew what would. A feisty carnivore. I saw a T-rex, it didn't look too happy. Then I realised I had forty-eight hours to find a way out. Then a pachycephalosaurus came charging at me! Just in time, I dodged out the way, then a pteranodon swooped in and almost killed me! Thank God it didn't.

A day passed, I couldn't survive any longer. I wandered around and found a nest of eggs. From how warm the eggs were, they must've been fine but the mum baryonyx came and chased me! It was about 8.5 metres long. I climbed into the treetops, I wasn't that scared of it because it was 0.6 metres long. I looked at the time, I only had fourteen hours left to figure out how to get back home. A velociraptor appeared, I tried to run away but it could run up to 50mph, hunting.

For some reason a carnotaurus came and swallowed the velociraptor whole but, before the carnotaurus saw me, I ran.

Before I realised, I tripped over a log and fell straight into a baryonyx pit! I tried to climb out, but I couldn't. Then I saw guns. I shot all the dinosaurs, but they were not dead. It was a sleep-timer bullet. Then I saw a note, it said 'Go to the watering hole, the portal will appear when the timer hits 0, so be there otherwise you will be stuck here'.

But I realised there were so many obstacle courses. I only had four hours left. I wanted to sleep, but I couldn't. It was 10 o'clock at night. There was a little stone. When I touched it, I had super speed. Then an ankylosaurus came out of the shadows and almost knocked me out, but nothing will stop me. Then a T-rex chased me onto this wooden bridge. There was a huge mosasaurus, it then swallowed the T-rex but not me. I kept on running and running till I was out of breath. "One more break," I said.

A velociraptor chased me to the watering hole. I know a triceratops is a herbivore, but it killed the velociraptor with its sharp horns. The timer reached 0 and I was back. "Finally!" I said.

Then I just slept and slept.

The next day, I woke up and everyone wondered where I was. To be continued...

Caleb Taylor (9)
St George CE Primary School, Great Bromley

Dreams Do Come True!

Dear Diary,

I just got home from school and my brothers are already making me angry. Oh... I wish to live in the jungle where there are no brothers annoying me. It is so quiet and peaceful in the jungle.

I couldn't sleep because my brothers were having a pillow fight, so I got my book. It was from the charity shop, so I didn't know much about it. Wow, it... it was glowing! Then a big blast of wind came and it took me through a portal. *Aaah!* Finally, it stopped. I was at the jungle!

Wow, it was so magical, I loved it.

Two days later, I missed my family. I would like to stay, but I have to go. Where is that book? Oh no, why is it not letting me through? What am I going to do now?

One year later...

The jungle queen!

Elsie Abraham (9)
St George CE Primary School, Great Bromley

Being Myself

Dear Diary,

There was once a boy called Dominic. He lived in a very small town and his family were very poor, so he would often starve because his parents didn't have the money to buy food. Dominic had just started school and he was very worried and shy, so he didn't make any friends when he started. Sadly, that carried on for about a year and then that's when it started! People started being mean to him because he had no friends and he 'wasn't cool'. Then, after a while, it really started to affect him. One day, his dad picked him up from school and he stormed to the car, feeling hurt from all the horrible comments he had received. His dad was very concerned about Dominic and politely asked him, "What's wrong, son?" and Dominic answered, "These horrible kids in my class have been laughing at me for not having any friends and being really skinny and, to make matters worse, it was in front of the whole school and made me feel completely humiliated and annoyed."

"Son, what do I always remind you of? You can be cool all by yourself and even if you don't have friends at school, you have me."

That's when Dominic had an idea. He would be himself and do what he loved most. He would write a book that would make him really cool and everyone would love him. He would spend hours and hours after school each day, carrying on writing a book and then making it better and better each day.

Finally, when it was published and the first book sold, he got so excited and then many more books were sold and, suddenly, he was the talk of the town. Then, one day, while he was out, he bumped into someone. It was the bullies from school and they said, "You need to give us some tips about how to write books," as that was what they wanted to do. "And you got motivation from our meanness."

But Dominic declined and said, "You were mean to me in the worst part of my life, so I'm not going to be nice to you, at my best."

Charlie Batts (9)
St George CE Primary School, Great Bromley

The Timer Of The Underground

Dear Diary,
One night, I was watching a monster movie. It was set in a forest. There was a grey machine, I did not know what mischief it would cause. Suddenly, the TV was pulling me forward, round and round. Suddenly, it stopped. I was in the forest. It was damp, dark and creepy. Suddenly, I spotted the machine. I walked over to it and looked at it more closely. It was a time machine! It had ten minutes to get out of the forest. I started to wander through the forest. I heard a rustle of leaves, then a great shadow appeared. It was a red wolf spider with the skin of a werewolf! It started to charge towards me, its fangs glinting in the moonlight. I started to sprint away. I heard its pincers clamping together.

I had eight minutes left. I had to find a way out. Suddenly, I saw a pile of big, wide pipes. I had an idea. I was going to trap the spider with pipes; yes, that was a good idea alright. Here we go!

I started to move a pipe, the spider charged. I jumped onto the top of the pipe, the spider ran inside. I secured it in, I had done it! I had done it! I have trapped the spider. Now to get home.

Five minutes left. Suddenly, without warning, the spider started to cry. Wow, I didn't know spiders could cry. I should set it free, but would it eat me? This was a hard decision to make, and risk-taking. But I had to do something. I slowly started to unlatch the pipe so that the spider could crawl back out. As soon as it came out, I jumped on its back.

Two minutes left. It charged to the TV, it jumped through to the living room, I had a spider in the living room! Quickly I reached for a torch. Must show the spider, show it to the TV. The spider jumped after it. I was safe. The timer had finished. Quickly, I turned off the TV. Phew! I had done it. I had protected myself!

The next day, I was in the Daily Report. For a week, I was front page. I was famous. I told my mum, she didn't believe me! But I know it's true!

Sienna Worn (8)
St George CE Primary School, Great Bromley

Wonderland Adventures

Dear Diary,

One day, in London, there was a girl called Lucy Rose and she invited her friends to visit London with her. They're called Scarlet and Charlotte. They walked around London, they went on the London Eye and went in Buckingham Palace. Someone had a car crash and almost died, and they were in the taxi behind! Their parents said, "Let's go back home."

Once they got home, Lucy Rose went to dance theatre school with Scarlet and Charlotte.

That day was fun but busy, Lucy thought to herself. She went to bed and had a dream soon she was performing at West End musicals! She dreamt she was famous, she lived in her own world. She knew she was going to Spain tonight. She was going with her two best friends in her apartment, and she wanted to do famous things with her two best friends because her mum always said friendship and family were all you need.

Lucy's mum quickly woke her up, she said, "Time to go to the airport, we are going with Scarlet, Charlotte and their mums, get ready." Lucy brushed her teeth and put on leggings, a dress and a cardigan.

Mum was doing her make-up and tying up her hair, put a dress on and a denim jacket, and walked down the stairs. "Put your shoes on and start the engine," and they went. When they got to Spain, something bad happened. Lucy's hand started glowing...
Scarlet and Charlotte and Lucy hugged each other and time travelled back to yesterday. They wondered where they were, so confused, and they let Lucy speak because they thought Lucy always had something smart she wanted to say.
"We time travelled."
"It is not possible."
"Maybe we are here to stop the accidents."
So, they did, all of them. They high-fived each other.
They were back, Scarlet said, "Now we have the power, we can do it whenever we want."

Isabella Rivas Long (9)
St George CE Primary School, Great Bromley

Stuck With Dinosaurs

Dear Diary,

I am Sophie, Sophie Hope Luke. My family look normal, but they are actually superheroes. My brother, Nowa, just got back from time travelling. Oh yeah, did I mention I have my own time travel machine? My family go on adventures all the time. Anyway, I have a story. Last Monday, it was crazy. We went on a dino adventure, we went back 5,000,000 years ago! We didn't stay for long, five minutes and twenty seconds to be exact. I said, "We should get back." We saw all dinosaurs, but one was near the time machine. Then *bash, bang, boom!* The T-rex had broken our time machine.

I started to panic, then noises came rushing near us quite fast. Dad and Mum were okay, they said, "Adios," and went to build a home. My brother took his camera, so he was just looking at his pictures. I was panicking. Luckily, Mum and Dad built a house.

On Tuesday, Wednesday, Thursday, Friday, Saturday and Sunday, I had had enough. I said, "No, no, no, *nooo*, I want to go home," when Nowa said, "Look, I found a pet!" It was an egg, a dinosaur egg.

I said, "*Mum, Dad!*" They saw the egg and *roar!* The gigantosaurus came stomping on me. "Help, help, help!" I said. "Oh my! Okay... Lalomazosababoom!" The dinosaur disappeared. "Can we go home now?"
"*No, we can't!*"
One night, I was bored to *death*, literally. I was vanishing... gone. "Finally," I said, "home." I started by being by the furniture. I started making a snack, then I started missing my family.
I started to vanish again and grabbed my family from a velociraptor. "Come on, *aaaaah!*" Then *poof!* I was home with my family. "Okay, *no more adventures!*"

Lilly Jeffery (8)
St George CE Primary School, Great Bromley

The Dinosaur Challenge

Dear Diary,
I am Daisy. Today was fun. My friends took me out for ice cream, but now I have absolutely nothing to do except for writing in my diary. My little cousin, Tom, he loves dinosaurs so much, he decorated the spare room covered in dinosaurs. It looked crazy and then I said, "Tom, what are you doing in my spare room?"
"I made something," said Tom.
"Is it related to dinosaurs?" I said.
"Maybe," said Tom.
"Okay, fine, I will come look," I said. I got out of bed and followed Tom. My footsteps were so loud, so I decided to tiptoe to the spare room. I was shocked as Tom opened the door. "A machine!" I said, in shock.
"Daisy, you mean time machine," said Tom.
"Yeah, yeah," I said. "So, why did you build a time machine?"
"So I can go see dinosaurs," Tom said.
"I think it's way too dangerous to see dinosaurs, you could be eaten by one, it's dangerous." He ignored me and went in the time machine. I had to go with him, it was too dangerous for him to go by himself.

So, I went in, we went back in time to the Jurassic era. I was already scared, but Tom started to walk away from me. I said, "Wait."
Tom said, "You coming?"
I had no option but to keep on going. I was scared about getting eaten. I just wanted to go home. I started to run so I could walk next to Tom because I was scared but, seconds after, we got trapped in a cage.
After one hour, we were out. We found a weird sign on a tree and I hit it and it opened a portal home, and we were just in time for breakfast.

Maddie Bateman
St George CE Primary School, Great Bromley

Evie's Dream

Dear Diary,

Once, there was a girl named Evie. She had a hard life. She lived with her mum, her dad and her famous twin sister who ran two channels on YouTube. Her name was Ava. Today, it was Ava's birthday which meant she would get more things than she already has. She got a £100 note to use when she goes shopping for clothes, she also got a puppy that she was told she wasn't allowed to share with Evie.

Evie doesn't even get any presents on her birthday; she doesn't even know if they know when her birthday is.

So, after that, she rushed upstairs into her room. She only has a bed, a lamp and a small carpet. She thought to herself, *it is better than nothing, I guess.*

"*Evie, time to go to bed!*" her mum shouted.

But there was a problem. Evie couldn't get to sleep. She said in her mind, *I wish I was like my sister. No one likes me at all.* Then she slightly closed her eyes and fell asleep, then something amazing happened. Her mum loved her. At night-time, she said, "Do you want to go to bed now or do you want to stay up?"

Evie said, "I want to stay up, but can I go and take my sister's £100 note?"
Her mum said, "If that's what you want, that's what you'll get!"
This was Evie's dream come true, so she snuck to Ava's room. "I have got it and I want to spend it." Then Evie woke up and realised that it was all a dream, but then she found a £100 note under her carpet, like in her dream. Now she was confused. Was her amazing dream actually a dream?

Emily Wainer (9)
St George CE Primary School, Great Bromley

The Diary Of Eliza Rose Green's Life

Dear Diary,

I was doing one of my comic strips whilst looking at my DogMan book for inspiration when my pencil broke. I knew my older brother, Ryan, bought a new pencil recently. I didn't know if it was any good though. My older brother, Noah, was picking up Ryan from school so maybe, just maybe, I could get the pencil. So, I crept out of my bedroom, I checked the hallway, the coast was clear! So, I quickly ran into Ryan's room, grabbed the pencil and ran to my room. When Ryan came back, he came to ask me if I wanted a snack and his eye caught the pencil.

"You thief!" he said and he ripped my drawing into shreds.

Later on that day, it was midnight. I was looking out the window in bed and there was a shooting star. I have always wished that I could see my future. I then started to feel pain in my tummy. My room started to disappear and I landed on a big double bed. I was an adult. Where was I? Where were my family? I was not Eliza; I was the other, future Eliza. I wanted my brothers; how old are they now?

When it turned daylight, I set off to find my family. I couldn't help but buy a chocolate bar from the shop. Yum! I was walking when someone said to me, "Nobody likes that chocolate anymore."
"So what?" I said.
"Just warning," said the person.
I couldn't find my family in the end, and all I do remember from my past is I will always be Eliza Rose Green and I will never, ever, ever give up, and that is one big promise that will never be broken.

Maya Varma (9)
St George CE Primary School, Great Bromley

The Empty House And A Missing Family

Dear Diary,

Today, I am going to finally ask my parents if I can get a phone. I don't care that they are poor; all my friends have one, so why can't I get one?

"Eliza!" screamed Mom. "Come down here now!"

"I'm coming, Mom," I said. I went downstairs and my mom was looking furiously at me.

"You went out with your friends instead of finishing your homework!" she screamed. "You're grounded!"

"What?!" I argued. "How? I hate you and I wish you would just disappear!" I screamed as I went upstairs.

I went in my room and jumped onto my bed but, suddenly, I heard a noise coming from my wardrobe. I opened the wardrobe door and there was a portal! A small one. I was going to close the wardrobe door when I accidentally fell into the portal. Suddenly, I was lying in my bed, everything was normal, except... I couldn't hear my family downstairs. So, I went downstairs, no one was there. I was alone, in my house, but it was empty, an empty house...

"It can't be!" I said. "Where are my family?" Suddenly, I had the idea to go outside. So, I went to the front door and opened it, I was in the middle of nowhere. I thought I was lost until... I saw a light on the ground. I ran towards it, but then I fell through the ground and I was back home! And my family were there. It turns out it was just a dream. A realistic dream... But I could feel every wall and object...

Lily-Rose Stoian (9)
St George CE Primary School, Great Bromley

Pearl, The Mermaid

Dear Diary,
One day, there was a mermaid called Pearl and her friend, Lizzie. They went swimming together every day in the ocean. They were like sisters, they loved each other, they did everything together and they played games together. One day, they were swimming in the ocean and found a magical land which has never been discovered before.

When they opened the door to the magical land, they found this glowing seaweed. They guessed it was magical, so they both ate a piece of the magical seaweed and, suddenly, the water glowed and took them to land, and their tails magically disappeared and they were human. When they were on land, they noticed their necklaces on their necks. They thought if they eat more of the seaweed, they would go home.

They explored more of the beach, then they wanted to go home. So, they ate more of the special seaweed and they went to the edge of the water. Three, two, one and their tails appeared again, so they swam back home.

"So, I guess we can go on land now."

It was only lunchtime, so they went home to get some lunch, then they played a game.
"Oh, it's bedtime, let's get some rest so we can have more adventures tomorrow. Goodnight."
"You too."

Millie Brown (8)
St George CE Primary School, Great Bromley

The Stolen Glass

Dear Diary,
I found glass camouflaged in the sand, so my guess is that it came from the ocean. I also found a shark tooth. So, I went home, excited, but my brother is mean. When I went to bed, I was holding the shark tooth. My brother thought I was asleep, so tried to take the tooth. I added it to my collection, and he told Mum and he was crying. Mum said you get what you deserve.
My brother kept on trying, but he got kicked in the face and I got a ruler and whacked him with it. Also, I was going to get a rubber and chuck it at him. I don't mind him keeping on trying because in a few more days his wisdom teeth will fall out so he won't be able to chew.
Next thing you know, I'm back on the beach but this time there was a portal. I jumped in the portal, I decided to be a monkey hanging from trees. I fell on my back and I had to get a tennis ball, so I went to the market to get an even harder and harder one.

Also, my brother went to get ten chickens because there were two T-rexes, so I threw four of the chickens and one punched the T-rex and hit it with a ruler and a rubber. I touched this stone and it gave me super speed.

Alfie Giles (9)
St George CE Primary School, Great Bromley

The Secrets Of Sailing

Dear Diary,

As I was getting ready for sailing, I caught a glimpse of my friends and I ran over and said hello, then we were called over to the boats and were told to stand around the square. There were numbered boats and you were given a number and you would have to wait for your number to be called. Then you would run into the square and say your name. Like 'Jane'. 'Jack'.

Now it's all done. Left, right, right... Yes, sorry, I was putting a sail in my boat, but now I have time to write. Now I'm getting my boat rigged, but then we stop for a walk. We say we have two hours and we go back to rigging our boats.

We are finally finished.

As I sail, I try to look at my friend, but I can't. So, I look at her through my sail and you'll never believe what I see...

"Aaaaaah!"

"What?" my friend shouts.

"You're a monster!"

"Hey! That's mean."

"No, it's not because you look like one!"

"No, I don't."
I look at her again. She looks normal...

Poppie Usher (9)
St George CE Primary School, Great Bromley

Diary Of A Day With Dinosaurs

Dear Diary,
When I woke up this morning, all I had was my bed. I went downstairs, I opened the door, I couldn't believe my eyes! There were ten dinosaurs! T-rex, velociraptor and loads more. I packed all my stuff but then, suddenly, the triceratops took me on an adventure. I couldn't believe my eyes again! There was someone on board with me, it was Mrs Sandell...
Then we went to school. I could not believe my eyes. Nixon was the only one at school. He got on a dinosaur's back and he could not believe he was riding a triceratops to the park. We went on the slides together, but the dinosaurs broke the other parts and it became one big slide. The T-rex hurt my dinosaur, so we went back to school and me and Nixon went home, to my house.

Melody Duffield (8)
St George CE Primary School, Great Bromley

Ghost Boy

Dear Diary,
I was sitting down on my bed, I was so, so bored. I only had a bed to sleep on. I went outside of my room and went down the stairs, *creak!* My mum awoke.
"Ghost Boy, back in bed."
"But..."
"No buts."
Up to my room I went.
In the morning, my mum shouted in my face, "Ghost Boy, you know better than that!"
"Sorry."
"Get out!"
"W-w-why?" I said as I walked through a wall.
"Bye," I said. "Grr."
That night, I, Ghost Boy, roamed the streets. After five hours and twenty minutes, I sat still on the floor and nobody knows what happens next...

Emily Brewer (8)
St George CE Primary School, Great Bromley

The Incredible Diary

Dear Diary,

I was playing a football game. We had a good opposition, luckily we got the first goal, but soon they would score, I knew it. They did, it was 1-1 then they scored again. We weren't going to give up though.

A while later, a friend scored to make it 2-2. Not too soon after they scored, but we still weren't going to give up and we scored again. It was my moment. I got the ball. I got past two, then another. I put it through another person's legs and scored in the top corner. My friends said it was a brilliant goal. Then the whistle blew and we won 5-3. Everybody was saying my goal was the best goal, even the opposition.

Fred Card (8)
St George CE Primary School, Great Bromley

Sebastian And The Cartoon World

Dear Diary,

It was 3am in my room, then a strange portal opened up under me. Then I ended up in my room again. *Strange*, I thought, then I saw an outline of a hand writing in pen. Then I went to my mum's room, I looked and... "I'm a devil!" I looked outside and Violet, my friend, was helping a whole bunch of cartoons, with a giant sword. I needed to go outside. Without looking, Violet threw the sword to me. Words repeated in my head. *First form, dead calm.* I said the words, "First form, dead calm," everything stopped. I saw a person made of lava laughing.

To be continued...

Sebastian Lord (8)
St George CE Primary School, Great Bromley

Diary Of A Footie Kid - A School Adventure

Dear Diary,

I was just moving into Year 4 at school when I found out what I was really doing - I was moving schools. I was thinking, *I won't see my friends again.* When I arrived at my new school I knew I needed to make friends quickly, otherwise I would be lonely.

When I entered the class I was told by my new teacher Mr Roberts to sit at a table. This table had me and three other people... Jason, Leo and Dave. I started talking to Jason and we became good friends. At break, we couldn't think of anything to do. We walked around in circles, minds spinning. I was no good with my big feet. No one even let me play because of my big feet. Was there something wrong with me? It was then a ball was kicked at me. I did a bicycle kick. Now everyone knows me as Footie Kid!

Ray Johnson (10)
St Mary's Catholic Primary School, Bognor Regis

The Incredible Diary Of Jenson Kelly

Dear Diary,

Day one

Okay, so I was on my parents' boat and we were sailing home. All seems fine, right? Yeah, until... I fell off the boat! Full of fear, I tried to stay calm but couldn't. I was drifting away until I saw my football. I clung onto it. I seemed safe, and yes, I was. Until I fell unconscious and woke up on an island. It was midnight, so I made a bed...

Day eight

Yeah, I know. I forgot to write for a *whole week.* I'll catch you up now. Day two: found food and water in a vast cave. Day three: not much. Day four: found my brother (now I'm not alone). Day five: found my bird, Paul. Day six: more food and water. Day seven: sent my parrot to find supplies. And we are back here. Recap of the day! Found a bed! Finally! About time.

Day nine is here and my brother said he was the one giving me food. All of a sudden, I saw a plane-shaped thing in the sky. I lit the fire and they saw it! I was saved! And that's my story.

Jenson Kelly (9)

Wansdyke Primary School, Whitchurch

The Incredible Diary Of Trixy

Dear Diary,
When I was two years old, my parents died in a factory. Ever since they died, I've lived with my grandparents! I was on a boat and, suddenly, it crashed. All of us survived, but we got separated. I was in a canal for four years, only with a fishy rod and a bottle of water. Before we got on a boat, my grandmother gave me a little snow-white sheep and I named it Cwtch! The little sheep reminded me of her! Then, suddenly, *bang!* The boat tipped over. I fell unconscious and dreamt of being with my parents. Suddenly, I felt something in-between my toes. I gasped for air as I looked around to see the most lush, golden, caramel-coloured sand ever. I shouted to see if anyone was there, but there was no response. I looked behind me and saw a tropical forest. My gut was telling me not to go in, but my heart said, "Go in, your family's peace and joy are there." So, I went in, hoping to find food and water to survive. Then I saw coconuts, a supply of food and water in the same thing. I wanted to make a shelter; you never know what is creeping up behind you! I had to do it before sunset. I found three big logs and nine big leaves.

I built as fast as I could until I got tired. I slept until the sun came up!

I was looking for more supplies. I found twelve more logs and ten more leaves. *Yes!* I did it. I made my shelter and then I heard someone call, "Hey, what are you doing here?"

I said, "I-I got stranded on this island yesterday," and he said, "I am warning you, be careful..."

That night, a tsunami came and then a boat. They let me on and I went back to my home, to my aunt and uncle. I never saw my grandparents again, but I am now happy as ever.

Holly Saunders (10)
Wansdyke Primary School, Whitchurch

The Incredible Diary Of Aliah Rose

Dear Diary,

I'm wet, sore and very fed up! This horrid nightmare needs to be over. I'll tell you what happened...

Me and my brother, Ash, are great swimmers, and Ash made a bet we couldn't swim to an island. So, we set up and got on our way. We were in our thick, salty wetsuits in the ocean. Ash dared me to hold my breath for two minutes. I was under for roughly thirty seconds but, due to my asthma, I passed out and started slowly sinking to the bottom... Ash dived down to try to grab me, but his heavy wetsuit pulled him down slowly with me, and he panicked and raced up, but used all his strength on grabbing me. We were both unconscious now...

I slowly opened my eyes, but regretted it because the sun was shining on my face. Wait, something dripped on me. I sat up and saw... "Luna!" I cried. Luna is our two-month-old puppy I got for my birthday. How did she get here? Why was she here? Is she okay? Was she injured? I had so many questions!

I saw Ash on his feet, calling for help. Luna slept in the shade. I saw some twigs in the shape of a den! "Den!" I cried. Ash looked at me blankly. "Look over there," I pointed. Ash didn't care. I called for Mom, she wasn't here... Wait! We were on an island! I almost cried. I thought about all my friends; my mum. I felt terrible and scared, but there was no one. We were stranded on a beautiful tropical island. I felt the worst. So, we had a sleep in case we woke up to Mum getting us up for a boring day at school. Actually, I'd do anything to be in school right now...

Poppy Rossiter (9)
Wansdyke Primary School, Whitchurch

The Incredible Diary Of Chloe

Dear Diary,

I was so bored, so I asked my caring parents if we could go on an adventure on a yacht. Once we hit sea, I get so excited because a new experience is always the best! I loved adventures so much that we would go anywhere in the world. Suddenly, my parents gave me rules on what to do and not... *I hated rules!* So, once they weren't looking, I peeked my head above the ocean. Unexpectedly, the yacht rocked slowly and I slipped... *I couldn't swim!* I tried to stay afloat, I was shaking in fear, *I can't explain how scared I was...* I saw an island; luckily, I was looking at the yacht to see if my parents noticed I was gone, they didn't notice... I was overthinking so much. *Did they even care about me? I will starve. I'm gonna die alone!* I sighed.

In the morning...

Yesterday was *soo* tough, it was very hard to sleep. I've been learning how to swim so I can eat crabs etc. Also, my cat, Tinsel, was with me. At least I have someone with me. "*I'm not lonely!*" I screamed. I'm still wondering if my parents noticed and are looking for me. Anyway, I dived in the sea, seeing a crab. I instantly grabbed it with all my might.

Well, that crab was tasty, I hope it's good for cats... OMG! I completely forgot the coconuts. I drank some. While I was walking, I saw some footprints, but I've never walked this far and then I realised... *someone has been here!*
Chloe and Tinsel.

Danika Newell (10)
Wansdyke Primary School, Whitchurch

The Incredible Diary Of Chloe Green

Dear Diary,

I was on a holiday cruise with my family. I went outside to smell the luscious air and the azure ocean when there was a big splash! My handbag fell overboard. It had my money in it. My heart pounded as fast as it could. What should I do? I decided to jump off the ship before my bag sank to the bottom.

Before I knew it, I was in the sea with my parents shouting at me. I grabbed my handbag and swam north until I reached an island with a sign saying: *Hawaii.*

Straight away, curiosity got the better of me and I started exploring. I crossed loads of trees and vines. Suddenly, I found a massive cave. I gently tiptoed in, just in case a jaguar was in there. I kept walking until I reached the end. Sadly and scarily, there was an Indian tiger. I panicked and tiptoed out.

When I came out I saw lots of bamboo. I carried millions of bamboo for two miles and built a shelter. It took me the whole day to build it with a place to sit and a place to store food. All I needed to do was put in comfy leaves.

I've been in Hawaii for two weeks. All I eat is eggs and drink pond water. I was on my way to find proper food like coconuts or maybe tropical fruit. I found a palm tree and started climbing but I got an allergic reaction so I rapidly climbed down.

Amina Kallamoqi (9)
Wansdyke Primary School, Whitchurch

The Incredible Diary Of Jenson Ashman

Dear Diary,

Monday, I was going to a football match in an aeroplane. As soon as something hit the plane, it crashed down onto a desert island.

I have found things to feed me and my dog on the desert island, and water for me and my dog. It's been hard for me.

I went in the woods, I found my dog drinking some water, so I climbed a tree and there was water for myself. I was drinking water and eating my fruit... There was a dinosaur! It got smaller and there were cuts on me. When it chased me, I fell by the plane with my dog.

No one heard me. I had to make sure I wasn't attacked more that day. After the dinosaur was stopped, I had to climb and my legs hurt. Suddenly, I yelped. *Crack!* We couldn't find a meal.

Crunch! There was another dinosaur inside a little shelter, so I couldn't rest in there. What a big dinosaur! it was really loud, it was like a dog after me and I didn't have anyone to help me to get me back home, to rescue, but I couldn't move.

I yelled, I couldn't do anything but wait, so I had to just climb when I heard a car but fell down. And that was from today.

Jenson Ashman (9)
Wansdyke Primary School, Whitchurch

The Incredible Diary Of Harry Barrett!

Dear Diary,

Today was an adventure-packed day. I was on a plane when all of a sudden the right wing fell off and caught on fire. Luckily, there was an emergency parachute so I safely floated through the air until I landed on an island. I was excited but also scared.

It was 9pm and I started to hear noises so I went to see what it was. It sounded injured. I eventually found it. It was a dog. It looked very hurt so I picked him up and took him to the little shelter I'd made.

I decided to call him Charlie. He was very dirty and looked like he had a broken leg. I decided to take him to the little pond to clean him up. I made him a leg rest so he could relax without hurting.

The next day, as soon as I woke up, I was starving. I needed to eat as soon as I could. I went outside to the little pond to see if there were any fish. Luckily there was! They were massive. I tried to grab one but it swam away. I tried to chase it but I fell in.

In the end, I was able to get it. I went to my little shelter and it ate it raw. "Eww! It's disgusting!" I shouted while laughing.

Harry Barrett (10)
Wansdyke Primary School, Whitchurch

The Incredible Diary Of Vicky Dover

Dear Diary,

I'm sick and tired of this island! I wish I was with my family, safe and sound! The next thing I know, I got stranded. There was nothing I had because it had nothing. What would happen now?

I could remember that I was having a soft caramel cake, then, after my dinner, I tripped off my family yacht. I was wrenched on this giant island!

At first, I felt confused for two hours, then I saw a dog and it looked like my dog, Flower. Then she noticed me and it *was* Flower!

Three hours later...

I started to get thirsty and hungry. I went to see the island, then I saw this little house, so I went to find a stick. I had to see it with my other dog, Stella. I was scared for my life... Stella was barking at the house!

I opened the door and found a man called Joe Pink. He asked me, "Who are you?" I said I was Vicky Dover, then he started to have headaches and stomachaches.

Friday, he gave me a drink and food. Then he told me how to live on an island with dogs. Then we became friends. Finally, I have a friend!
By Vicky Dover.

Starla James (10)
Wansdyke Primary School, Whitchurch

The Incredible Diary Of Delilah

Dear Diary,

I woke up on this surprisingly warm island. I opened my eyes, expecting to see Emma right next to me but she wasn't. I stood up in terror. Then I heard a bark from the other direction. My jaw dropped when I saw Emma. She was all wet and fuzzy...

Let me explain what happened... I have a dog, her name is Emma. I was on a yacht and I was playing fetch with Emma. I threw the ball a bit too hard and the ball landed in the water. Emma started running to the end of the boat. I shouted but before it came out she was in the sea. I was scared. I was screaming in terror. I jumped off the boat and into the water. I just started sinking. I must have been so scared. I ran out of oxygen and that's all I remember.

When I got washed up on the island, I got up and saw Emma. She was okay. I picked her up and started to explore. I found a tree with dead leaves for a bed and some tropical fruit like pineapples and watermelons but I couldn't find any water.

This was going to be a long ride.
Bye, Delilah.

Annalise Quirks (10)
Wansdyke Primary School, Whitchurch

The Incredible Diary Of Charlie

Dear Diary,

Day one

I am enthralled by the view of this wonderful destination on this beach. What else is better than this? This is somewhere I couldn't ever dream of; it is a paradise for me. I wish someone can just share it with me.

Day three

I have been waiting for someone to find me on this beach, but now I am doubting if anyone is going to find me. I need to explore. I started walking and walking, but when I saw a startled monkey in a palm tree in the middle of the wilderness, I was starting to think this wasn't a beach. This had water surrounding it; it must be an island. I think I need to find shelter because I am going to be here a long time!

Day four

Today, I am going to start making shelter. So, I am going to try to find a lot of sticks. This is terrific. Let's start building!

This is going well. That's finished off now, let's go in it. *Crash!* Oh, what a disaster.

I am determined to make this my home.
Charlie.

Dolly Lewis (9)
Wansdyke Primary School, Whitchurch

The Incredible Diary Of Sam Dani!

Dear Diary,

Ever since my family died, I have been so lonely. I wish I could have saved them. It's all my fault. Anyway, I'm here to tell you about my day.

I came onto this island that nobody has ever seen before. I'm so lucky it's me. I found a new fruit and of course, I named it Samsuko.

This island was full of adventures. It almost made me forget I was lonely. One thing I absolutely hated about this island was that I hate water. The feel of it just made me want to gag. I hate gagging! Ugh!

Earlier, I cut my leg on a massive rock. How did I miss it? It's bigger than me! Luckily, when I'm older I want to be a doctor so I got that problem out of the way by using leaves. I don't know what I should name the island though. Maybe Samduge... I'm not sure, but I'll figure it out.

Today I tried coconut for the first time. I know, I'm very picky but I loved it.

Well, that's all for today. I will see you tomorrow. From Sam.

Lilah Taylor (10)
Wansdyke Primary School, Whitchurch

The Incredible Diary Of Ben Hills

Dear Diary,

I have had just about enough of this island.

It all started when Chloe (my twin sister) and I fell off of the family cruise and washed up on this island. The first thing we did when we woke up was search for food. Luckily, there were lots of tropical fruit like coconuts and grapefruit. After that, we found a pool of fresh water and went to sleep.

A couple of peaceful days later, we woke up to birds screeching, which was weird because they're normally singing. But I just moved on. I woke Chloe to do the daily things like collecting more food and water. Although the island was luxurious, I wanted to be saved and Chloe did too. So, I collected sticks and made a fire. This also brought fish into the food equation. After all this, I got tired, so I went to sleep.

When we woke up, the birds were screeching again. Then I looked up and saw why. There... was... a... volcano.

Ruuuuunnn!

From Ben.

Max Stenning (10)
Wansdyke Primary School, Whitchurch

The Incredible Diary Of Nick Jive

Dear Diary,

I am stuck on this mysterious island. I wish that this was a nightmare and not real life. Since my mum died on the boat, I think that I'm the only person alive in my family.

After that night, I heard someone singing in the distance. Then there was a huge bang coming closer to me. I was standing still when I heard a breath on me. I turned around and saw a group of tigers trying to attack me. Suddenly, a volcano erupted and scared the tigers away. I heard a growl far away. I just ignored it.

When I woke up, I was trapped in a cage. My heart was thumping like someone playing the drums. I was so scared but I was lucky. I was free from this trap. I ran but my worst fear came along... snakes. I screamed and called for help but I knew nobody would come and get me so I just ran and cried for hours. Then I stopped but then I saw something in the sand...

Effy Coombs (10)
Wansdyke Primary School, Whitchurch

The Incredible Diary Of Camren

Dear Diary,
I am getting tired of this 39° weather. I am determined to go back to 24° because it is cooler and I'll stop sweating so much. The water is dangerous near America because there are dangerous sea animals. I was so scared especially of the sharks because they have sharp teeth like a knife. I will stay on the hot sand.
The next day, it was 31°. I can't help it. The sand is soaked but at least it is cooling a bit. But as the day went on, the temperature got lower and colder and the next day it was -2°. I had a new blanket. I was shivering.
The next day it was -10°. The sea had icicles in the water. Then the day after, it was 17°. It was much warmer. It stayed at 17° for a long time and it was much warmer so it was much better.
At night, the temperature was 15° so still warm like a blanket.

Stan White (10)
Wansdyke Primary School, Whitchurch

The Incredible Diary Of Alana Myles

Dear Diary,

I have just been on a beautiful ferry boat. A huge, colossal wave hit the boat and everybody stayed on but me...

I am now on a tropical island loving life! I have already been surfing and swimming in the sea! It's now day two, but I am starving. I couldn't sleep last night because of how hungry I am. I am now waiting for someone to come and help me find where to get food. I shall take a nap until someone helps me.

Day three... I've just woken up with a note next to me telling me to go inside the forest and there will be a surprise. I headed into the tropical forest... I couldn't believe my eyes! A cafe! I ate pancakes and coconut iced drinks. Mmm!

Day four... I walked outside of my shelter. All of a sudden my family were there to rescue me. We got on an aeroplane. I got into my bed and went to sleep.

Alana.

Roux Harris (10)
Wansdyke Primary School, Whitchurch

The Incredible Diary Of John

Dear Diary,
I hate it here. I've had enough of this horrible island. Especially after what I have just realised. I went up the volcano and saw the lava bubbling... This could only mean one thing. It was going to *erupt!* I ran down, back to the hut, as fast as I could. I found Jimbo hiding in the trees of the jungle like it was hide-and-seek. He just stared at me as if he knew what was going to happen.
I picked him up and drew a huge *Help* sign in the sand. When I saw a speck of something in the distance. It was shaped like a boat. I waved my arms in the air and did everything I could, but there was no hope. They went right past me and disappeared into the distance. I fell down on the sand and stared into the sky, then I saw smoke clouds...

Spencer Dix (10)
Wansdyke Primary School, Whitchurch

The Incredible Diary Of Trixy Tayh

I am dying! Just a week ago, I was caught in this tropical terror. At first, I was scared but also calm and relaxed but now that is over.

For three days now, I've been tracking a mysterious creature, monkey, gorilla, orangutan? Days without food, finally water, bread and even a coconut. Silver, my silver-grey husky, didn't stop barking for even one second. We are a helpless couple who now, more than ever, need help.

Days on end without luck, have been looking for a way home. Would you like to know what happened? Well, three weeks ago, my family and I were sailing across the Black Sea when suddenly, out of nowhere, a wave, a humongous, black wave, crashed into us and there we were floating along. Oh no! Night-time. I must go. Bye!

From Trixy.

Izzy W (10)
Wansdyke Primary School, Whitchurch

The Incredible Diary Of Tom

Dear Diary,

I am stranded on an ominous island because my friend's boat brought us here. I was trying to sleep, along with my friend, Jack, when all of a sudden we heard rustling and bushes shaking. All of a sudden it stopped dead.

We investigated and what we found was a massive feather resting on the cold floor. We both stared at each other in shock and silence. We both quickly made a fire so people could find us and we could keep warm. The huge feather was next to me. I tried not to think about it though. I couldn't sleep so I sat and talked to Jack.

The next morning, I woke up and made a sandcastle for fun. I got some fresh mangoes from a tree and finally, had no stomach ache. Will we live?

Evan Hudd (10)
Wansdyke Primary School, Whitchurch

The Incredible Diary Of Lilac River

Dear Diary,
I am Lilac River from the USA and I was walking in the forest all alone. I fainted for no reason and got taken by a stranger into a boat. I woke up in the crystal-clear ocean. Well, it was kinda pretty but it was deep enough for the boat to float away.
The stranger was explaining all about the crystal-clear ocean.
"This is an important ocean, so you got to be really careful."
I got this feeling that I would get seasick by the long ride so I said I might be a bit too seasick. I calmed down and breathed in and out whenever I got the shivers. I managed to survive by doing that.

Tessa Bowering (10)
Wansdyke Primary School, Whitchurch

The Incredible Diary Of Reno Lacey

Dear Diary,

Last night I was on a plane on my way to America. Suddenly, there was a big crash. Silence occurred. I woke up and looked around. I was aware of a noise. I marched my way over.

"What's this thing?" I muttered.

I picked it up and dusted the beak off.

"I'm awake!" it shouted.

"Argh!" I screeched.

It was alive. I instantly shut it.

"Mmmm!" it muttered.

The next day, well, midnight, I woke up. Food was provided and water too. It was lovely. I hadn't had any in ages.

Reno Lacey (9)
Wansdyke Primary School, Whitchurch

The Incredible Diary Of Michal

Dear Diary,

I have been on this island for two weeks and now we've met someone else on the island.

When Bella and I went to get coconuts in the evening, we saw smoke in the sky. I didn't know there was another campfire on the island.

When I looked, there was another person on the island. He was really hungry so I climbed up a palm tree and got a coconut. For the first time, I smashed it with my bare hands. Then I gave it to the man. He liked it. We went back to the cave and I introduced him to Bella and he liked her.

Michal.

Libby Pope (10)
Wansdyke Primary School, Whitchurch

The Incredible Diary Of Rob

Dear Diary,
Last night I was making my way to Hawaii when I heard fierce waves crashing above my face. All of a sudden I opened my eyes and realised what had happened.

After a while, I started to explore and I thought to myself I could possibly be here for a while with no one in sight. I stood puzzled as I wondered how I had got there. I wanted to see what more could happen to me on a stranded island. I was hungry and I looked far away with a feeling of what was going to happen next.

Reid Griffiths (10)
Wansdyke Primary School, Whitchurch

The Incredible Diary Of Roux Lewis

Dear Diary,

I have been on the island for days. I have been looking for food for three days. All I found were coconuts all over the floor. I have been living on coconuts. I'm going to find something to make a sign so I can get out of this island and eat normal food. I am sick and tired of being here. I want to be in a normal house. I hope I get out of this place. I am going to build a raft and try and get out.

Hallie Thompson (10)
Wansdyke Primary School, Whitchurch

The Guard

Dear Diary,
This was the day, the first day I arrived at the prison camp. Watching, watching the souls of the poor people slowly go lifeless. They all stood in a corner in a bunch, cowering. The emotions I was feeling from that moment showed in my face, even if they weren't meant to. Later on, a few guards went to a different camp, leaving me the only guard left. Before they left, they informed me that more guards were coming to help keep all the 'prisoners' where they were supposed to be. When they took off and there was no sign of them, I slipped some leftover food I had in my bag and carefully placed it in my hand to give it to the prisoners. Very small smiles grew on their faces, while others were too shy and traumatised to give any response. Every time I had the chance, I repeated this process. That was until day five. My mind was set to something more challenging. I was going to end this cruelty. The guards had to go again. I was not a 'good enough' guard to go anywhere.
When they were gone, I found the key and let the prisoners out. The joy showed on their faces. No one knew how long they had been there.

One person waved at me and then ran away. As they all ran away, the new guards came. They looked at the open gate to the concentration camp, the prisoners running for freedom into the deep forest, then me.

I got sent to another concentration camp and no one will ever know what is actually happening. Never will I understand why this cruelty is happening.

Goodnight.

Indie Williams (10)
Woodlands Community Primary School, Upper Cwmbran

Stay Hidden

Dear Diary,

I'm Miep, thirty-three, and not a believer of what they do to the Jewish people. I have a steady boyfriend, Jan, and he always just nods when I rant about how I feel towards the Nazis. He always leaves for work, comes home and doesn't say a word.

I guess I'll start with my day. My job is to help hide the Franks, a Jewish family. I'm not a maid, I help because they're Jewish and I want to save their lives. This week, because of my loyalty to them, they invited me to dinner with them. We had rations. We felt uncomfortable because there were Nazis shouting loudly outside. I recognised a voice. I tiptoed towards the window and saw none other than my boyfriend in a Nazi uniform. I ran to the attic to hide in the corner. I quivered when I heard a thump on the floor. I slowly locked the hatch but I knew they'd heard it...

Suddenly, Jan was hunting through the dusty items that crashed around. He found me hidden. "Stay hidden," he said.

They left. I sprinted downstairs to see everyone had gone.

Evie Rostron (10)
Woodlands Community Primary School, Upper Cwmbran

The Strange World!

Dear Diary,
I woke up this morning and wasn't in my bed. How strange! How weird! How peculiar! Instead of being in bed, I was outside and everything looked weird, as though I was on a different planet. The sky was emerald-green, it looked beautiful. I looked down and the grass was yellow and it had black spots. I started to walk to explore, then I heard a voice, a tree was talking to me. I could have sworn it said, "Beep, beep, beep." I was shocked. I felt something watching me. I looked over my shoulder, it was a flower. I rubbed my eyes to check and it was looking at me.
I started to walk along the path, when I came across a lake. Suddenly, a fish jumped out and started flying, it was amazing. After that, I looked to my left and there was large field. Something was off. I looked again and there were cows playing. How peculiar. Then I remembered before I was there, I was lying in my bed before I had appeared in this strange world.
Then I woke up to my alarm clock and the song 'Wouldn't it be Funny' was playing.

Calon Griffiths (11)
Woodlands Community Primary School, Upper Cwmbran

David's Journal

Dear Diary,

Today I was playing at a local park in Neukölln with my brother, mum and dad. We were playing football together. I was very happy to be with them. Dad was in goal and we were taking shots. At the end of the field, I saw a bunch of soldiers walking towards us. I was worried because on the news I had heard that Jewish people were being arrested. They told all of us that we had to be relocated because we were Jewish people. Mum and Dad were angry at the soldiers.

Before long we were all on a very big train with a bunch of people we didn't know. Me and Tyler were both petrified. There was no room on the train because there were so many people.

Not long after, we arrived at some sort of camp. We were all dragged off and told to line up and wait. After, we had to get our hair cut. But we also had to give our jewellery.

Then this young soldier pulled us to the side and said that we had to escape because otherwise, we were going to be killed. Me and Tyler were both emotional.

Holly Furness (11)
Woodlands Community Primary School, Upper Cwmbran

The Boy In The Bubble

Dear Diary,

Today I had to eat boring food again. I hate the food, all it is is a piece of bread and water. I want something better like pancakes or anything really. Mum went out so I just looked out my window and had an idea. If I snuck out to look for food what would happen to me? I just stuck my head out the door of the bubble and I was fine.

So I went downstairs and ate some food. I was so relieved nothing happened so I stepped outside. It was so cool. I liked it but then all of a sudden I started to fly. I was scared at first and didn't know what was happening but then I heard screaming so I rushed to it.

Some people were screaming because someone was hanging off a building so I helped them back to safety but then my mum got back and saw I wasn't there. I zoomed back and then I got grounded because she didn't believe I actually came out of my bubble. However, that night made me realise I didn't need to live in the bubble anymore.

Maddison Williams (11)
Woodlands Community Primary School, Upper Cwmbran

My Last Hours

Dear Diary,

It's day ten of being stranded in space. As the rocket loses oxygen, I can feel the air getting thinner and thinner every day. I don't think I have long left, I have lost all contact with anyone on Earth. All of my resources have almost run out. So basically, I was doing my usual routine that covered most parts of the Milky Way. But on this strange day, something peculiar occurred. Out of nowhere, another rocket came zooming past as if it was out of control. I had never seen it before so I decided to follow it to see if it started to slow down, as if it didn't it would crash going at that speed. Was it friend or foe? As I started to follow the rocket, I noticed it was speeding up so to keep up with it I started to go faster as well. After about twenty minutes of chasing it it started to slow down, but I didn't realise and going at those speeds we were going to collide. Luckily, I swerved away before, but it scraped the side of my rocket.

Jack Higgs (10)
Woodlands Community Primary School, Upper Cwmbran

SpongeBob SquarePants

Dear Diary,

Hi, I am writing to you tonight on this showy type of day because yesterday I had the worst day of my life.

Firstly, I was woken up at exactly 3am because my pet, Larry, wanted his breakfast. Then I needed to go to work which is at the Krusty Krab. Then after that, I accidentally poisoned one of the Krabby patties so I got fired.

Later that day, Squidward came to my house and told me off and said these very words...

"SpongeBob, you squared boy, leave everyone alone."

But then I gave up and I didn't speak to anyone. Then Patrick (my best and dumbest friend in the world) offered me to come to his house and have a sleepover and as usual I said yes. We did party games, football and we even stayed up all night! After that best day of all time, everything went back to normal. I got my job back, Squidward was my friend again and Larry had his new collar and it made him sleepy so no more waking up at 3am for me anymore!

Lola Ralph (10)
Woodlands Community Primary School, Upper Cwmbran

Pink Gets Up And Carries On

Dear Diary,

Today wasn't one of my best days. It started off not so good as I woke up this morning with a cold. My throat felt like I'd swallowed razor blades. I couldn't take the day off because today was the first performance of many in Germany. After resting, I was getting ready to perform the first date of my tour.

Hearing the roar of 75,000 people screaming my name made me feel overwhelmed and excited to perform. I was then helped into my acrobatic harness by the production crew (who's done this time after time) and then was ready to go, not knowing how close I was to the edge of the platform. I slipped and hurt my back.

At this time my emotions were going through my head, discomfort, pain and embarrassment. I was also feeling a little angry as my fans would have seen this all over the world, but as the strong, independent and focused woman I am, I took it on the chin, got up and then started the final track on the stage.

Neve Eyers (11)
Woodlands Community Primary School, Upper Cwmbran

The Incredible Day

One winter's morning in July, we boarded the Sprite of the Sea, in search of the migrating humpback whales. We'd been out just over an hour when a call came over the radio, another boat had spotted them. We rushed over to the location to find them. We sat there quietly in anticipation, waiting to spot one of the beautiful creatures. Everyone was rushing from front to back, hoping for that special moment when one popped out of the water. Then we heard the words we'd been waiting for - "They're over here!" Out of the clear blue water slowly came two humpback whales all covered in barnacles close enough that we could touch them. They started to roll and splash almost immediately, knowing they needed to put on a show for us. Then from nowhere came more of the pod to join them, but before we knew it they were gone.
Wow, what an incredible experience that I'll never forget.
Ffion.

Ffion Mason (11)
Woodlands Community Primary School, Upper Cwmbran

My Not-So-Normal Day

Dear Diary,

It started off like any other morning, by snoozing my alarm until I ended up missing the school bus... So I had to walk.

After I arrived, the headteacher gave me a detention. At least it wasn't a suspension.

After I finished all my work in maths I began to walk down the hallway past all the lockers while talking to my friends until I stopped short of my locker. I thought I saw something... It was a small hatch which was designed to blend into the wall. I decided to investigate but I was stopped right in my tracks. It was time for my detention. I'm not sure what sort of secrets lay in that hatch. There might not be anything at all.

After I got home I had dinner before looking at floor plans of the school and I couldn't find anything... I guess I will have to keep investigating tomorrow...

Goodnight.

Ethan Watkins (11)
Woodlands Community Primary School, Upper Cwmbran

Albert Einstein's Greatest Fault

Dear Diary,

Today was an extraordinary and unforgettable day in my life. I can't believe I can say this, but I have just been notified that I have been awarded the Nobel Prize in physics. This was for my efforts in creating and researching the photoelectric law.

In the morning, I was going through my monotonous routine when out of the blue a phone call suddenly came. On the other end of the phone was Professor Carl Wilhelm Oseen, who informed me that I was chosen to be the winner of the Nobel Prize. I was gobsmacked at this fact. I have to deliver a speech to an audience and explain how much of an honour it is. Then there will be a banquet in my honour.

I am ready to receive the Nobel Prize and hold it for the very first time. As the day comes closer I realise how lucky I am.

Rylee Alexander (11)
Woodlands Community Primary School, Upper Cwmbran

Simon And Britain's Got Talent

Dear Diary,

Today, me and Bruno had an argument.

The day started with me having my daily green smoothie and then saying bye to my beloved fiancée Lauren. Then I drove in my BGT car to pick up my fellow judges.

When we arrived we walked down the red carpet then Ant and Dec drove behind in a Tuk Tuk. After we walked in, Bruno kept talking when the producers told us to start so I asked him politely to not talk but he didn't listen, so I had to shout at him and then I got angry and he just stormed off. Then Amanda and Alesha stayed backstage with PJ and Duncan (Ant and Dec) because they didn't want to get involved but in the end, we made up and became friends.

What will old BGT bring for me tomorrow?

Simon Cowell.

Ellie Titcombe (11)
Woodlands Community Primary School, Upper Cwmbran

Is This A Good Idea?

Dear Diary,
It's day thirty-two of our 'journey'. At least the captain calls it a journey. It's more of a wander. We don't even get a lot of money. But at least we're fed. The Anke (the Anke's our ship) isn't very nice to people like me. I feel sick on the upper deck. The captain says we're almost at the 'Kraken's Den'. I'm pretty afraid, we'd rather find nothing and waste our trip or find... the Kraken. We don't even know if it is a large sqiud like it has been depicted, no one's survived to see it. Anyway, I'm ending my entry here, I need to help on the upper deck.
(PS if you're a crew member peeking at this journal, I am Ta'n.)

Caleb Owen-Smith (10)
Woodlands Community Primary School, Upper Cwmbran

The Miracle In The River

Dear Diary,

It was a rainy day and the windows were completely drenched. My father, although he didn't want to do it, took us for a walk. We were extremely excited! Eventually, we made it to the river. Our father sat near the edge and threw stones in the river.

Suddenly he lost his balance and fell! We both started to chase after him but we knew that we couldn't save him because we didn't have hands. Then out of nowhere lightning struck! Unknowingly we had got powers! We both flew up and used our telekineses to save our dad! He was amazed.

For the rest of the day, we spent our time saving lives!

Rhys Evans (11)
Woodlands Community Primary School, Upper Cwmbran

Bob

Dear Diary,
I woke up this morning and had a strange feeling. It felt weird. When this happened I was in my house and then I turned purple and yellow. This happened about 100 times more. When I turned purple I ate a cat, parcels, cases and more! This is the worst thing that has ever happened to me, but I don't know if my friends have it too...

Riley Parfitt (10)
Woodlands Community Primary School, Upper Cwmbran

Young Writers Information

We hope you have enjoyed reading this book – and that you will continue to in the coming years.

If you're the parent or family member of an enthusiastic poet or story writer, do visit our website **www.youngwriters.co.uk/subscribe** and sign up to receive news, competitions, writing challenges and tips, activities and much, much more! There's lots to keep budding writers motivated!

If you would like to order further copies of this book, or any of our other titles, then please give us a call or order via your online account.

Young Writers
Remus House
Coltsfoot Drive
Peterborough
PE2 9BF
(01733) 890066
info@youngwriters.co.uk

Join in the conversation!
Tips, news, giveaways and much more!

YoungWritersUK   YoungWritersCW   youngwriterscw

Scan me to watch The Incredible Diary Of video!